Break The Heart's Anger

BY PAUL ENGLE

BREAK THE HEART'S ANGER
AMERICAN SONG
WORN EARTH

PAUL ENGLE

Break The Heart's Anger

Paul Engle
1961

DOUBLEDAY, DORAN & CO., INC.

Garden City   1936   New York

PRINTED AT THE *Country Life Press*, GARDEN CITY, N. Y., U. S. A.

☆

DEDICATION

Now in the running body of lean space
Hangs the world like an enormous heart
Beating through arteries of light the pulse
Of day and dark, that is the pulse of men.

Out of that heart I come to you with hope,
I, a newer Lazarus from the living,
To tell you strange things I have seen today
Even with these same eyes that look at you.
Be not frightened if the angry smell
From the dark cave of earth where I have lain
Four days is on me, or the cloths of life
That are the leaves of oak and human faces
Cling to my arms, or that my tongue exult,
For it has tasted sunlight and the rain.
All who have stared until the dreaming mind
Was bruised with darkness, blinded by its sight,
Let my eyes be crutches where you lean.

We live in a century that cut its throat
The second year of its life, a foredoomed child,
And yet behind the knife was not its own
Fumbling hand that knew not what it did,
But inescapable and gathered forces,
The death struggle of twenty centuries

[v]

DEDICATION

That were one single mood of the world's time,
The taut nerves writhing with terrific force
On the gashed hills, and yet the exaltation,
The screaming rage that was another birth,
A dream and a defiance in our hearts
Pale for all the blood that flowed away
But knowing the first tremble and the thrust
Of life that from the marrow of our bones,
Deep from the ultimate dark human strength,
Will flow to veins and take the beat that is
Our human lunge against eternity,
Against the shape and fury of our doom,
Breaking the teeth of time with a long arm
Leaner than light and harder than despair.
Now, though yet the white days of our life
Drool from our mumbling mouth and simple words
Stick in our throat, I call to you across
A length of ocean, narrow as an inch
Of mind between the eyes:
                              America,
I hate you so because I love you so,
I who have walked barefoot across your hills,
Swum your rivers and with a shy hand
Touched fields of corn in Iowa and felt
Earth turn beneath me, through your haunted
          towns,
The way and wildness of their streets, have cried,
When the last wind has worn my face with touch
Bury my heart at Forty-second Street
And Broadway, the Times Building for a stake
Run through it like a crossroads suicide,

[vi]

DEDICATION

There at the busiest corner where no rest
Will come, the subway wheels will cut my bones,
But that will be a kind of peace, knowing
That there is no rest either for my land.

I cannot think of you and all the dreams
That wandered through your life and were as real
As living persons with a voice and name
But all the begging shadows of your men
Walk with their dragging feet upon my eyes.

Do you think, America, you can forever
Walk the thin and tight-rope edge of time
With the umbrella of a silver dollar?

I give you this because my hands in you
First broke the wind, my eyes first bore the sun's
Fury and the stare of men.
                              To you
Also who took the earth between your hands
As a child a butterfly in a white net
And gave it to me, saying, Let it lie
A moment on your finger while the wings,
Cut from pure light, quiver, and it rests
Being tired with flying.
                              In the dreamless dark
Your face was like a little fire and all
Your body living shadow under it.

Not with hands take this. Look. I put it high—
The spike of a hawk where wind hangs, and my
    heart.

Gollenshausen, Bavaria.

[vii]

☆

CONTENTS

[ix]

CONTENTS

[x]

PROLOGUE

☆

AMERICA, bastard child from all the world
Born, yet parentless, hard scrapper beating
Your lone way out from a child into a man,
It is not strange you were cocky, forever carried
A chip on your shoulder, boasted the length of the
     earth
You were one tough baby, hard as nails, swaggering
The streets with chin stuck out and a grin,
     shouting,
Take a poke at that, kid, if you're lookin' for
     trouble,
I'm half mountain lion, half Texas steer,
With a dash of rattlesnake and horned toad, taking
Easily in one jump and a yell the land
From the Blue Ridge to the Big Horns, and
     wearing
The whole damn Mississippi for a belt.
I'll pull my right shoe off and kick the moon
Clean over God's left shoulder for good luck.
I'm the world's original playboy—look me over.

Because you thought you had a date with a dame
Called Easy Money, for a thousand years,
You took the immeasurable cloth of time
And used it for a rag to shine your shoes.

[3]

BREAK THE HEART'S ANGER

Nation of Jacks forever with a laugh
Climbing the cloud-lost beanstalks of your build-
     ings.

Your whole life a perpetual song and dance.

And yet in Washington I've heard you crying
Because, having been barefoot so long, your feet
Sprawled in the dirt, their flat toes toughened, now
You must wear leather shoes, forget your marbles
And that bright penny of your youth, once spent
Over and over, fallen out through a hole
In your pants pocket, lost in the orchard grass
Where you hooked apples at night, throwing a stick
Up to the heavy branches, or in the crumbled
Swimming-hole bank, under the roots, downstream
The cattle lowing belly-deep in the water.

You strode the earth, not with a lifted sword
But a gleaming piston rod of power in your hand
Till not alone the world but even yourself
Was blinded and believed its dazzling glare
The very flame of glory, till you found
On a grim morning with the east wind turned
Suddenly cold and full of rain, you bore
A dog-uncovered bone in your hand and beat
Madly, a tin drum with colored pictures
Like a child's dream of going to the wars.

Evenings in Dakota where the dust
Fell week-long in a Pharaoh curse from the sky
You sat on the front steps, smoking your pipe,

[4]

PROLOGUE

And turned, for the first time, into yourself
To trail your heart's interminable prairie
For the shy, untrapped meaning of your life—
A day-old track on a hill, a few flank hairs
Caught on an elm, a wild-grape-hidden spring
Muddied with drinking—found it fled, and nothing
But your heart's enormous hollow, arched with
    sky.

And when (Upper East Side) you bought fresh
    fruit,
New potatoes, a bunch of flowers for the wife,
In the street market of immortality
You found they shoved your money back and said,
Sorry, buddy, that's no good here, it's all
Streetcar tokens, slugs, lucky pieces,
Chicken feed, nothing behind it.
                  America,
You minted out your soul in alloy nickels
Faced with an Indian, backed with a buffalo,
And spent it in the dime store of mad dreams.

In Florida, where the white cranes cry over
The deep Everglades, bull alligators
Bellow up the moon, I have seen, swell-headed
    youth,
The head-hunting Amazonian women,
The avenging fates of overspeculation,
The logical height and end of your dead system,
Shrink your bloated skypiece to a fist's size
And fight for who should wear it on a string.

[5]

BREAK THE HEART'S ANGER

The country's become a morgue now, I've gone up
To the county coroner, asking, Any bodies
Found on lower Broadway, in Cicero,
From nigger knifings, gang murders, dope raids,
To be identified? Here's one, he said,
The suicide squad brought in an hour ago,
And pulled back a sheet—Christ, he cried, it's
    breathing!
It was you, America, you living corpse,
Your throat grinning from ear to ear where the
    razor
Had ripped, but somehow missed the jugular vein.
Your eyes closed with dollars before you were dead.

In Colorado where the columbine
Leans its purple breasts to the prairie wheat
I have seen your screaming eagle with the lightning
Arrows gripped in his claws, the broad wings bent
From Oregon to Maine, touching two waters—
O vast wingspread of a continent, a nation
Huddled in its shadow—become a sparrow
Pecking the gutter-horse dung for old oats.

I pity you, tumbleweed land, wind rolled
Over the heat-cracked plain, caught in a fence,
Having not the wisdom of uprooted grass
That, bearing the sun's cruel knife blade at its
    throat,
Will yet beat down into the iron earth
The hot, white rivets of new roots, to hold
Till the rain come and deeply harden them.

[6]

PROLOGUE

How pitiful now, who once so proudly ran
Through time in seven-league boots, the blue
    bandana
Of the west wind knotted at your throat, fiddling
The whole world up to a dance, with old Dan
    Tucker
Or the latest Yiddish blues from Tin Pan Alley,
Slapping the lean butt of death and shouting,
Come on, baby, scrape that frown off your face.
Kick 'em out, girlie, high, wide and handsome.

You Saturday night nigger, drunk on his pay,
Whistling at midnight past graveyards to keep
His courage up.
                You we have dreamed would climb
The rock and glacier of an American peak,
Rainier or Pike's, throw off your clothes to stand
Naked in the glare of history,
And while your body bore the sky and took
The sun for heart until your veins ran light
You would sickle down the rich, full-kerneled
    winds
Of heaven with the bright blade of a song:

    Whether early or late
    Letting my eyes pale or darken
    In morning or evening light,
    At sea level walking
    An Alabama swamp, the night
    Barked trees, or deerlike
    In the Alleghanies stalking

[7]

BREAK THE HEART'S ANGER

The lost Boone trail,
Or in Chicago tearing
Roosevelt Road, cutout wide,
Booze in the back seat, the wail
Of sirens around me where I cannot hide—

I have been the gambling nation,
Glad to sit in an alley
With that blue-gum nigger
Time, crooning of his gal Sally
And Gabriel's salvation,
His hands on the ivories slow
But quick on the trigger.
Spit on the dice, win or lose
Rattle 'em high, rattle 'em low,
Seben come eleben
Baby needs a new pair of shoes,
Easy come, easy go—
And singing a new kind of blues:

Now in these days
Plunging the dark wood,
The Arapaho
Timbered mountain, I blaze
The ax-bruised bark for a way,
And scream when I raise
The ax again and find
I am the hacked trunk, the gray
Scar is my heart, the blind
Forest my eyes, the unpathed
Mountain of earth and mind
All one trail, wider than day.

PROLOGUE

From the Jim River, the Sangamon,
Nueces, Fox, I will drink
The rain-blooded water and swear
In my coming, to be, to think,
There is a truth, one that I wear
Like a brand-new pair
Of pants in Spring—
Movement, the will, the can
Force of moving, to say
I don't know where I'm going
But I'm on my way.

I will make a new song of the word,
A proud song, big in the lungs,
A free-for-all, everything goes,
Part barber-shop, part jazz,
Part cowboy, all American tongues,
A hill-billy's Jew's-harp itchin' the toes,
A Georgia fiddler givin' the razz
To 3 A.M., and a muted sax
Moanin' deep till all the world's
Swaying and swinging and making tracks
For Joe's Quick Lunch or Harry's Place,
Buck Tooth's Barn or a Harlem dive,
For the first time told that it's alive
In the new-word song of a new-world race.

America, long wind blowing,
For you not moving is not being,
Moving is being, is going
Lightly on nerves' feet
Where touching is seeing

[9]

BREAK THE HEART'S ANGER

But only singing is knowing—
The thing become, fleeing
From beginning into flowing
Is the word become song.

Here where the long
Compass needle
Of a continent points north and south
I will shout in the Blackfoot Hills
With an American mouth
The song of my tangled wills
That will be to my twisted heart
Deep rain after drouth
When the dry creek bed fills—

Being for me is moving, quiet
Is not being. Here in the tall ways
Of sun-shafted buildings, the steep
Wind riveted and roofed till men fly it
With vertical, square wings
Is movement's heart, the deep
Core of being where man sings
Restlessness out of his head
And walks the long curves
Of earth, pure being, unled
Through the dark streets of his nerves.

Here, walking Broadway or wide
Michigan Boulevard, hitch hiking
The Lincoln Highway, here
Has the word moved like the tide

PROLOGUE

Of a plowed field in the earth,
Moved into man and become
Boned and blooded, and cried,
Now by a terrible birth
Are the word and man one.

I, with my feet in the corn
Of Illinois where have run
The hard heels of the plow,
And my heart in the eagle-torn
Peaks of the Rockies, will fling
To the glaring face of the sun
The proud defiance of man—
Here is the word, I will sing,
Become a life and a line
And to you where we all began
I hurl it back as a thing
New in the world, a sign
That the next storm wind will bring
Of a slang and a song where ran
In the earth the American ring
Of a word, the American man.

Yet we have heard nothing save the tiny cry
From a narrow street, of a child who wept because
Having cut his finger, seen a drop of blood,
He thought his heart had burst.
                              You have no time
To sing, you are forever running away
Shrieking, lest you hear or understand
The lean, avenging fury of yourself.

BREAK THE HEART'S ANGER

And I have seen you, O poor Job of nations,
Now because you had a boil on the neck,
Being so long clean-blooded, down on the dung
    heap
Flung, to beat your breast and tear your hair
And hurl up dung into the eyes of God.

But you are not alone, for all the world
Cries, Pity, with you. Every nation stares
Into the other's face, into the sky,
The guts of a bird, reads a deer's thigh bone,
Looks in a mirror for a way, to find
Only its own reflected, helpless eyes
Begging and frightened.
                They are all diseased
With the fever of wretched government that burns
And wastes the tortured flesh till it cannot sleep,
With the racking chill and ague of too much money
In too few hands. It is only the life-patient,
Deep, man-haunted earth that is not sick,
Gentle in cropped fields.
                Now I hear in the night
Rise from every corner of the world
The life-tormented yell of starving men,
From doorway beds or subway benches, wrapped
In newspapers—*Beauty Engaged, The Hardware
    Jones'*
Leave For Europe, Agitator Jailed.
The toes of children rip through old shoes and
    scrape
On the hot streets or in the deep snow. Women

PROLOGUE

Lift up their eyes, no longer filmed with patience,
In the question that is their birthright and their
    curse:
Here are my children, thin, the bones begging for
    food,
There are no more quarters for the gas meter, no
Credit at the butcher's, the heat turned off.
Here is a man glad for a chance to work
Hard, long hours, overtime, and yet
Must walk the streets or sit in a cold room.
I am a woman. I do not understand.
But has a man no more the right to work,
A child to eat? A woman at evening
To rest in her family without the fear
Morning will find them turned into the street
With a handful of clothes and an old chair?
                                    This is not
Your way, America.
                        Yet now I see
In Alabama cotton burned, in Iowa
Hogs slaughtered and buried, in Montana
Wheat plowed under. While ten million men
Shiver and hunger. This is not your way
America. Remember—if one man eats
While another starves, his very food is cursed.
The bread line is a rope will strangle you.

You've kidded yourself too long, America.
It's time you looked the straight fact in the eye.
The world's gone bust, gone haywire, and you
    with it,

BREAK THE HEART'S ANGER

You, the infallible, spoiled child. Fate's got
Your number, buddy, he's got the dope on you,
Either you act now or he'll slip up and say
You're through, fella, you're done, washed up,
    cold,
Out on your feet and you don't know it, you're
Dead from the ears up. Scraaam.
                         Remember
That living men do not forever crawl
Down in the gutter and die in sight of fire
Which burns the bread stuff that could nourish
    them,
That there is an ancient power in the world,
Blind and cruel and terrible in act,
And it is not in the stars or in your eyes
That you alone of all the world's lands will
Escape the unimaginable fury
Of the lean-bellied, too long patient poor.

You've panhandled your own people, you've be-
    trayed
The faith of a hundred million, the deep soil
That lengthened your skeleton, the nervous wind
That lifted your cheek bone, the dream of men
A hundred and fifty years ago, who looked
At a thin line of towns by the sea's edge
Huddled, up the tidewater to the first
Lean mountain, and said—

                      Here is a new thing.
Here is another twist of life in the world's
Lift of men to the sunlight. We have torn

PROLOGUE

A new son from the tired guts of Europe,
Cut the navel string, left it here on a strange
Shore to suckle on maple sap and milkweed,
Grow up half wolf-boy and half god, to thumb
His nose at a far home he has not seen.
Here is a new people—
                    America
You have betrayed that people.
                              This is a shame
That not alone will leave a white, ridged scar
Over your cheek, will let your name taste rotten
On tongues that spit it out, that scorn to speak it,
But can destroy you.
                    You will wake one morning
To hear the relentless hounds of hungry men
Crying destruction over your doomed hills.

O desert nation, jackaled with your dreams.

Yet there is a way. This is not the Alamo,
The walls taken, the Mission entered, fighting
Hand to hand with the Bowie knife, Crockett
Fallen at last in a roomful of his dead,
The relief held beyond the flooded river.
It is the old American way, the going
Tough, no salt, tobacco wet, the weak
Clamoring to turn back. It is another
Cumberland Pass, the guide shot and scalped
In sight—sound—of the camp, the narrow trail
Dark with the forest death.
                          It is a pause
In the long war dance of our history, a turn
Of our life. Either we go on to shout

BREAK THE HEART'S ANGER

The great blood cry, or slink away to the squaws
Taunting in the buffalo tents, the boys
Making lewd gestures of us in the ponies.

We live darkly in the world's great darkness
Ringed round on the leaning hills with a fanged fire
That in the gray, bird-crying hour of dawn
Can run through the dry grass to leap and tear us,
Rip the lodge poles down, consume the pemmican
Dried for winter, all the old and sick
Left screaming on the black ground, and a few
Escaped to the mountains with a medicine bag
And a knife, to live on roots and bark, and die
In the first blizzard, bones piled in the Spring
For the friendly buzzards. Or we can ourselves
Crawl up in the night to steal it from the gods
And carry it in a pouch to our own valley,
Fuel it with the dead and broken wood
Of a society we have proved rotten
And found the courage to destroy. O then
Having built up that man-exalting land,
The clear expression of the human thing
In the social multitude and in the lone
Individual with his single way
That is our self-created destiny,
It will become the true American flame
That will be deep fire in the nation's eyes,
That will burn steel but will not burn our hearts.

                                    Kitzbühel, Tirol

[16]

FOLK OF THE WORLD

So, BIG BOY, you've been taken for a ride,
Blackjacked, dumped in the gutter, left to die,
And you don't like it much, you're sore, yet afraid
Of squealing to the cops, or another gang.
Remember, they had said, one peep out of you
And there won't be no second time, if you know
What's good for you, you'll keep that big mouth
      shut.
Mum's the word.
                  Yet come with me where earth
Is tattoed all over with men and women
Like an old sailor drunk in every port
Taking from each on chest or arm or leg
A naked woman, wriggling when the skin's pulled,
A fish, or a lucky word, and we will talk
To strangers in all places, saying, Friend,
Have you got time for a drink, just a quick nip
Standing at the bar?—Here's looking at you—
And see what in hell it's all about, the shouting,
The hunger, the men jailed or underground
Where no habeas corpus will get them out,
Or any bail.
                  First in our own land
Where the dark and straight-haired skulls are not
      yet cracked

BREAK THE HEART'S ANGER

With the iron weight of history, driving
The old wilderness trails, or newer concrete,
Paddling a birch canoe on the rock curving
Lonely rivers of our blood, to find
A footprint on the sand bar, covered ashes,
Still warm—look in a snow-blind trapper's eyes,
Ask a lost Indian, daft with an empty belly,
For the road out to the first post, taking
Our way by the grass, tips pointing south, stalks
Lighter green on the north side—or with
An old Ford rattling west, at filling stations
Looking at maps, getting a quart of oil,
Asking the best route over the ridge.

                                       Or go
Wandering down a road in Minnesota—
Ojibway runner, the silver wampum belt
Of lakes flung over the green robe of your pines—
Or Kansas, walking between two mighty hands,
The flat heat over and the flat land under,
To stop and ask a farmer, What's it all about?
You, Jake Reinheimer (blood and name of the
       Rhine
Dwellers in the vineyard-terraced valley),
Or you, Rudolph Holub, sad for the Czech
Pigeons flying the valleys north of Praha,
What do you think of the world's bellyache,
You who feed that hungry belly?
                                  Later
Over the gull-ghosted Atlantic, Europe
Running her wrinkled, lecherous thin hand
Over the full breast of America,

[20]

FOLK OF THE WORLD

To speak with many men in many tongues
And humming a little, a child's kind of song:

Will you on any plain
Or by wave-warped lake beach
Cry, when you feel in your neck
The twisted fangs of my speech?

You who have power in vain,
You governments built on a wreck.

You whose scheming and strain
Are but the pitiful reach
Of an armless man, feeling
In dream old elbow and wrist
Bend, in the moonlight bleach,
And leans to pick from the wheeling
Floor in his groping fist
Book, or shoe, till kneeling
From bed he falls and each
Arm fades to a shoulder twist.

For I will rip you with words,
Long-tusked words that can tear.
If you lock yourself in a room
You will find the dark and the door
A more dreadful doom
For I will be there
And you will not see me. Now
I walk in the open sun,
In the fields of daylight where

BREAK THE HEART'S ANGER

The furrows cut by the plow
Are ropes from the coiled earth spun
And with them I'll rope and throw you,
Hog-tie you, and when it's done
Spit in your face and say,
Don't struggle, nation, I know you,
You, and your furtive way,
Sucking the hearts of your men—
But soon they will rise, their tread
Will trample you down, and then
Their gathered cries will flay
The north wind till it blow you
Shouting over the head
Of the rolling moon, and when
You cry but once will sow you
Deeper in earth than red
Nevada rock, or the grave-hungry dead.

Poor folk of the world
Wherever I go you
Cry for a greater light
Than the dark now has hurled
A moment into your sight.

If I find it now I will show you
That flame when the dawn-thin, bright
Comb of the day has uncurled
The thick black hair of the night.

Freiburg-im-Breisgau

GREAT VALLEY

GREAT VALLEY, hung like a hammock, from the
    eastern
To the western mountain ranges, lashed and tied
To the Catskill and the Colorado peaks
By the sinewy, taut arms of telephone cables,
With the long legs of your rivers hanging over,
Platte, Miami, Ohio, Cedar, you
Granary of the world, the nation's pigsty,
Throwing your railroads a thousand miles with a
    flip
Of your hand, grabbing the waist of America
In your fist and shouting, Come on, old girl, we'll
    dance
Till the roosters crow and it's milking time.
                                        Farmer
Proud of his big barns—so high, in autumn
Clouds under the roof and rain falls—of soil
Black in the bottom land, the rich hills topped
With the brown dust blown clear from Wyoming,
    proud
Of cattle bred till their milk flows nearly pure
Butter fat, Jerseys and Herefords, a child
Can put his fist in the deep hole over their eyes,
Of corn bred out of the Indian maize, lifting
So tall men are lost in a field—the children

BREAK THE HEART'S ANGER

Watch the new planted hills come up like fresh
Grandmother quilts knotted with green rosettes
And shout the old Iowa song of growing corn—

    If it's planted in May
    With the sun all day
    It'll be knee-high
    By the Fourth of July—

Proud of his farm machinery, hard workers,
Gang plows, disks, corn pickers, gold-flowing
    threshers,
Of those husky farm girls, silos, thrusting
Their round hard bodies higher than the barns,
Filled in the autumn with chopped fodder soaked
In molasses till it ferments with the odor
Of gathered walnuts and all through the winter
Gives off a drunken breath—moslem pigeons
Pray to the east from the iron roof.
                    At night
Coming up from the last chores he sees
Air mail beacons turn on the horizon
Like a nervous child twisting its buttons, planes
Heard high over, and seen, the faint lights flying,
Lost birds carrying a great roar on their wings—
Denver, Omaha, Iowa City, Fort Wayne,
Prairie crows, hunting the windy land—
Wapello, Sac, Red Wing, little lark towns
Nesting the tall grass.
                Farmer glad
For the oatmeal he sends all over the world,

[26]

GREAT VALLEY

The luck of his calves at county fairs, for sows
Fattened till they can't walk, for his speed
At husking corn.
               Earth being, equally
Proud of his tractor and the long loam it tills.

But I have watched an old American thing
Walk again in the earth—the stride of men,
Long and easy and free, the hunter's swing,
Lighter on leaves than the fox, good for all day—
Men who carried a hate and a curse and a fire
Deep in their crying hearts. In the hot dawn
I've watched them, naked to the waist, holding
A hand-woven blanket over that fire,
Signaling the caught smoke out in warning puffs
From burning hill to burning hill, over
The prairie, beyond the Catskills, over the sea,
Around the world and back again to the hills.

They sang a new way and a new belief,
Their voices deep with the earth's grief:

    Here is a new song out of the land,
    Blowing clean from the west
    With the taste of mountain air
    And the grit of Dakota sand,
    A bitter thing that will spare
    Not father or son, nor rest
    Till once again the hand
    Of hate has taken the knife
    And carved from the crying breast

BREAK THE HEART'S ANGER

A rib of hope and a brand
New heart for a new life.

We have not marched all day
In the Mojave waste
Where the wheels break, the gray
Eyes of children go black
And the oxen low for the taste
Of sweet water again
Till the bull whip's bitter crack
Beats them on—the horn-hafted
Whips that have blinded men
And broken a neck or an arm—
On where the gold-head, wind-shafted
Arrow of sun cuts brain.
We have not known the strain
Of the fearful night alarm
When the feverish watchers feel
The greasewood trunks are guns
Or the mirage where runs
The mockery of rain
Like a blur of angry rust
On the clean horizon steel
Till they meet, and the wagon train
Drinks with the belly's reel
The intolerable dust.

Yet it is ours, the land,
The plowing, the planting, the reaping,
Butchering the winter hog,
Slitting its throat with the hand
That had torn it out of its sleeping

GREAT VALLEY

And found it the brood sow teat,
Ours the felled oak log,
The bob sled frame carved out,
The ears torn in the sleet,
The rabbit hunt with the dog.

What you forget, we shout,
Is our land, the sour and the sweet.

It is not that you have betrayed
A state or its men or a city,
It is our soil you've framed,
A put-up job, with your paid
Hands that have less pity
Than death, that would be ashamed
To act towards its own as you
Toward those who come to birth
In this land, blooded alike, and named,
Like eyes, hazel and blue.

You have betrayed this earth.

This patient power that flamed
In time untold to the new
Heat, and bright as a knife
Gave out like an uttered word
The lean shape of life
To roam the length and the roar
Of the wind like a frightened bird
Crying and blind, before

BREAK THE HEART'S ANGER

The sun had heard its cries
And with keen-edged light for blade
Burned in the quivering bone
The little match flame of eyes.

Let the wind wail with no
Troubled man to hear it,
The fences fall in the snow
Drifted, with none to fear it.
Now it is better so.
Drive all life over the edge
Of a Colorado canyon,
Let none leap as they near it
Down to a foothold ledge
To live till the eagle beak
Hurl them down to the long
Lingering death of the weak
Or the quick death of the strong.

When one man hungers and cries
For food in a land where corn
Is burned, the wheat plowed under,
A nation is doomed, the flies
Of fate will crawl on its mouth
Till the ancient, awful thunder
Of half-starved hate arise
To break with a terrible wonder
That land from north to south
And pull the night over its eyes.

GREAT VALLEY

Accursed American land,
Hide your face with your hand.
You have betrayed the earth.
It is your doom's birth.

Chiemsee, Bavaria

CHICAGO

☆

Cyclop face of Chicago with the long
Michigan eye in your forehead, from the heart
Of America looking deep into that heart,
And out where your farthest nerves reach—Bur-
    lington,
Great Northern, Union Pacific, Pennsylvania.
Grim face, hard in the eye, cauliflower-eared
From too many scraps, nose bashed in, the boys
Winking, saying you're punch-drunk and half
    dippy,
Hair in a mess, the lake wind in your hair.
Face glad for the set of its jaw, white teeth,
A singing jazz tongue, dancing feet.
                              Blunt face
Speaking with Western lips a Western speech
Quick and jumpy and coarse, full of strong words
Ripped out of the earth.
                         Your blue eye blazing
With the flame-clean and wild American light,
Narrowed with staring at enormous space
From the Gulf to Great Slave Lake, from Buffalo
To the Sioux-haunted Black Hills.
                            Stockyard steer,
Long boned, Brahma horned with an eight-foot
    span,
Unroped, unbranded, tossing your head, beating

BREAK THE HEART'S ANGER

Earth with feet slim for running, tail
Stiff up in warning, roaming a continent
For range, the sweet grasses and water holes
Known, the trails between.

                    You, Chicago,
Are the most native city, with your mingled
Bloods of the world—Polack, Bohunk, Wop,
Kike and Chink and Greaser—you are most deeply
American-blooded, with Boston half English,
Tucson half Spanish, New Orleans half French.
You have come up out of the Western land,
Mushroom town—the sun at evening
Behind the Rockies, rain in the night, morning
You stood here by the lake, the Indians
Not yet all gone beyond the troubled hills
Where cabins burned and the blond scalps were
    taken.
Squalling child, dirty behind the ears,
Yelling that you were hungry with a big belly
That would take a lot of groceries to fill,
Jumping from toothless baby gums to buck teeth,
From milkweed juice to raw corn whisky. Skyline
Tall and long as a tasseled August cornfield
With rain and a hot sun. Taking your gangs,
Sawed-off shotguns, pineapples, the armored
Booze cars and the milk and laundry rackets
As a mongrel dog his multitude of fleas,
To be scratched, but yet a necessary part
Of being a young pup who always slept
On filthy straw in alleys, too damn busy

CHICAGO

To do more than lift his tail and bite.
Your history so brief you've written it out
On the palm of one hand.

                  Strange new being, born
Out of the prairie loam, from every land
In Orient and Europe, taking the lake
And the crow flight measured plain as little things
To play with for an hour, cracking the hard
Hearts of your toughest men like hazel nuts
With bare teeth.

            To you life says, Step on it, kid,
Or yesterday will be kickin' you in the pants.
Tomorrow's a dollar I give you. Spend it. Have
A good time. Don't let it burn a hole in your
    pocket.
You South Side Jew holding once a month—
All Stock Must Go, Gigantic Sacrifice—
A fire sale of the heavens, goods marked down,
Stars half price, comets under cost,
Lots on the moon, lake frontage, for a small
Down payment.

           Town of the true American voice
Mingling the lark cry and the L roar.

                    I know
Under that skyscraper, ribbed with girders,
Gold-gilded chest of yours there is a heart
Big as a barrel.

           What has come to you now?

I've heard you say to the girl friend suddenly
Out of laughter, Come on, take off your corset
And have a good cry, you'll feel better then.

BREAK THE HEART'S ANGER

I've watched you spit out the rot-gut gin and
    scream,
It's not more stinking booze I want, nobody
Got a slug of good water, anything that'll knock
A fifty-year hangover?
                     You've rooped the suckers
Out of their last plugged dime with "gilt-edged
    stuff"
Not worth the paper it was printed on.
But now they've got you, big boy, you've been
    slicked
At your own game, and you can't take it standing.

Faustus town, you have signed your soul away
On the dotted line one night when you were drunk,
Soused to the gills, so boiled you couldn't read.
Now when it's time to pay they're beating your
    door
And yelling, Come on, Come on. We know you're
    home.
You're three installments behind. Either we
Collect this time or take your soul back with us.
You can't put this one over on the world,
It's taken all your lip it's going to take.
Open up. Open up.
                 You who have regretted
Only all life that you had left unlived.

Your grain board, your public utilities
Have jipped the public blind, you've always given
The Middle West the dirty end of the stick.

CHICAGO

But they're on to you now, you've gambled just
Once too often with quick money played
Against human misery.
$\qquad$ You can't
Buy the earth on margin forever.
$\qquad\qquad$ Nor think
Dawn and twilight, east and west horizons,
Are nothing more than mighty slot machines
Where you drop the sun and moon to get a handful
Of playing slugs, worth two bits each in trade.

Pitiful people, you poor shaggy bear,
Dancing with an old tin cup for pennies
With the chain of stupid government on your neck,
The sidewalk biting your feet.
$\qquad\qquad$ When will you rise,
Get some backbone, can all this whining talk
That fighting's no use, better throw your guns
Under the table and drink till you're there too?
How did you get here? Because your fathers stayed
At home over a mug of beer? Or because
They took life in their hands and shaped it out
As chance and their own will would have it,
$\qquad$ steerage
On the Atlantic, bundle of clothes, a new
Speech cutting the tongue?
$\qquad\qquad$ Can't you remember
The whoopee days when you jumped on the tables,
$\qquad$ shouting,
It's a great life if you don't weaken?
$\qquad\qquad$ Now
You grovel like a Barcelona beggar

BREAK THE HEART'S ANGER

Showing his green sores to the world.
                                        I've seen
The wind in December come from the bitter lake
To rip your people up the back, and women
With a few papers crouched by cellar windows
Where the thin heat stuck its head out, nigger kids
Crying at the white knife on their black skin,
Your soup kitchens crowded with men who lost
Their job, their decent clothes, their self-respect,
And soon will lose their patience—these are not
Beasts, peasants, serfs, but American men
Who always said, One man's as good as another,
Take off his pants and shirt, and give him a bath,
With an equal right, whether he's got a million
Or two bucks in his jeans. And when they do
There'll be hell popping on State and Madison.
It won't be fun to look at, plenty of
Nice people are going to get hurt.

                                        It's not
Alone your living men you have betrayed
But the new world idea of a man—
Here, at last, were John Doe, Abe Kalinsky,
Tony Rocco, Pierre Montreux, to have
An even break, those who came with hope
Of getting at last a chance to start all over,
Kicking the past into a corner, stand
With head up, look every man in the eye,
In a land where it was always a new day,
Yesterday wrapped in the garbage and forgotten.

CHICAGO

Now you give them this one chance—to live
Under the mean hand of charity
A sort of half life, dressed in other men's
Cast-off clothes, and in the land of greatest
Hope, die in greatest hopelessness.

I have heard in you, Chicago, mocking town,
Men sing in their hearts, mumble on their tongues,
A song quieter than all the crying
Of your cold and hungry people in the night,
Glad for the chilly dark to cover them,
And yet more terrible than the tongue-ripping
Shriek of a dog hit by a car, the shout
Of fire-trapped cattle, because they cannot see
The force that runs them through with the tearing
    spit
Of losing a job, turning them slowly over
A bread line fueled fire as the barbecue
Of a town that sold its honor and its men
That a few may pile up gold in the guarded
    vaults—
A job that never will come back until
The society that bore them, beat them down,
Knows, like the April dogwood, that a new
Time has come, and what the rain is for,
And brings out budded leaf and branch and flower
Over the old and deeply groping roots.

Despised and by yourself doomed city, living
On the memory and dribblings of a dream:

BREAK THE HEART'S ANGER

No more run, Chicago singer,
When work is done
Over the long
Prairie wind
On feet of song.

Let the antlered sun
Hook one hard prong
Under your town
And fling it over
Lake and dune,
Corn and clover,
Till it lose its heart
And even its name
And its men are hurled
To every part
Of the wandered world
From whence they came.

Let the eager lake
Tear down its towers
To the beach and break
The stockyards, free
The cattle to parks
Where the fled mowers
Will leave them be.
Let time pull down
Its walls, the larks
Haunt the air
Of this mad town
That once would wear

CHICAGO

The gathered hours
Caught in its hair
Like prairie flowers.

If one man stay
In the town alone
To prowl the rubble
And look all day
In the tangled stone
For his heart's trouble,
Let him go at noon
To the lake and drink
One last cup
Then flee from the sedge
And the ruin's stink
To the prairie's edge
And string himself up
In a hickory tree
With a tough rope
Made bitterly
Of his lost hope.

If such a man be
And does not die
By the deep lake mud,
His heart will turn
Caustic, his blood
Thicken to lye
In his veins and burn
The flesh away
Till but the bony

BREAK THE HEART'S ANGER

Frame, lit with day,
Runs in the stony
Field, where rain
Covers in pity
With grass and grain
What was once, men say,
The pride and pain
Of a tall city.

Let the green corn
Write on the land
From which was born
Towers tumbled down,
In a twelve-foot hand
Their curse, their bitter
Words of doom:

Here was a town—
Now a litter
Of steel and rocks
In a fertile field
Where the cricket mocks
The earth unhealed—
That hung its men
On a golden cross
To double the yield
Of watered stocks
And cut the loss,
That minted its men
Into thin dimes
And spent them wildly

CHICAGO

In what were then
Madly and mildly
Called "good times."

Let your name
That now men know
Only as shame,
Be again a low
Indian village
With beans to hoe
And arrows to fashion,
Where is no pillage
By paper and pen
Of goods and life
Nor any passion
To take from men
With club and knife
What one man needs
Less than another,
Nor give of the earth
The richer, younger,
Back to weeds
When from his birth
One man hunger
More than another.

Let the squaws sing
To the growing seeds
In the fields they till
With bone-made harrows,
Let the wolf fling

BREAK THE HEART'S ANGER

From the wind-worn hill
Into the sky
The unfeathered arrows
Of its fanged cry.

Eze Village, France

CALIFORNIA

HERE THE American runner of the lean
Wilderness lope, swinging, day long, light
On the trailed earth, following the high
Cloud lifted west the length of a continent
Halts by the wave edge and stares into the sun
That he has hounded from another sea
Under a colder sky. Here now the runner
Lifts three times to that waning sun the broad
Wampum belt of his country, interwoven
Blue of Rainy Lake, red of Huron
Iron lodes, gold of Winnebago
Mottled corn, then hurls it gleaming out
Into the drowning water and lies down
On the warm beach to rest.

                    O Indian girl
California of the brown breasts, long
Limbed, clean flanked, round armed, with eyes
    bluer
Then the grapes of your hills, walking through the
    surf
On eager, laughing feet, letting your hair
Fall out behind you to the meeting winds
Of east and west, one with the mountain tang
Blowing down from the big trees and bare rock
Sweetened by orange groves and vineyards, one

BREAK THE HEART'S ANGER

Beating in from the loud interminable water
With the salt breath and the kelp taste, shrill
On the gull tongue.

Bend your neck, for no
State like you where the rich earth is deeply
Deliriously blooded with a life
Could hold its head up to the scornful moon
Or the hard winds of heaven, when there are men
Who cry for what that earth can fully give,
Who roam your too quick, flowing gold-built cities
With face and belt drawn tightly up in hunger—
Los Angeles, city not of angels
But of tormented ghosts; San Francisco,
Where poor Saint Francis, with his birds and
     flowers
And the power of God streaming into his heart
With the sunlight, would find his quiet place
In a soup kitchen line; Sutter's Mill,
Where the yellow clay challenged the world to come,
And the world came, around the deadly Horn,
Over the dry desert where, they say,
The heat burned out the tongues of lizards.

There
In one word is the history of our land.
Burn up your textbooks and on one white page
Print in high letters that glittering word—
     GOLD.
When the Fourth of July orators get up
To shout, "The noble ideals that have made
Our great nation," hurl them down and brand

CALIFORNIA

That livid word on their forehead until
They cry it out themselves—GOLD. But add
That many men were braver than the gods
In seeking it.
             You have made of our whole
Land a mine—shafted with the broken
Bodies of emigrated workers, many
Knowing not in our language simple words
Like food and sleep and woman, calling them out
In strange tongues—with your eyes forever fixed
On the pay-dirt lodes, the assayer's test, the piled
Ingots, till the smelter fires burned out
The red from your blood, and all your arteries
Ran black mine water, your face and hands
Turned yellow in the world's eyes, till you cursed
The sun because you could not smelt it down
Into pure bars of gold.
                    You've been proud,
California, of your swank hotels,
Your millionaire beaches, of your real-estate
Promoters taking a few sandhills one night
And next day building a town, your fruit valleys
Irrigated, your oil wells and the faked
Oil-well stock. You shouted, We have crammed
Two thousand years into one century;
Christ was crucified in Yosemite,
Next day everybody had a Ford
And drove to the park to see the carved skull hill,
Leaving their pickle jars and sandwich papers
Where the Roman spearmen diced and Mary
    watched

[51]

BREAK THE HEART'S ANGER

Sight fall from the limp eyes to earth.

                                        You can't
Be so damned cocky now, with your skin games,
Your loud mouth squawking your climate, when there are
In San Francisco riots, hospitals full,
Three hundred in jail, police mobbed, dock strikers
Clubbed and gassed, but once again the land—
O rich, long swinging, proud American land
Of twelve-foot corn and breast-high wheat, you earth
Where there were once men glad to plow and reap
In a new way of life, breathing new air—
That land made safe again for Democracy:
Democracy, where individual man
Has the inalienable right to starve,
To lose a job and never get it back,
To have his pure identity as man,
A thoughtful creature, powered with a heart,
Mocked by stupidity of those who hold
Control of things with hands that are cut off
Clean from the wrist, although they cannot see it.

Meanwhile, at Washington, the big chiefs grunt,
Leap naked with a writhing snake in their mouth,
Beating a drum and chanting to call down rain
On the heat-cracked fields where gourd vines wither, corn
Sears in the hot wind.

                                Now the American dream
Roams the land as a living nightmare, that

CALIFORNIA

Which once had been the symbol of our life
Over us gleaming like a flame, has turned
Into a curse. That which made us great
Has made us grovel. We have been proud to say,
I am of this land. But now, if the world asks,
Why so wretched, all the laughter gone
Out of your mouth, light from your eyes, hope
Out of your beaten shoulders? we can say,
We are American. They will understand.

California, wake, before you are
Murdered in your sleep. Have you forgotten
That when it rains in the valley, on the peaks
There is drifted snow, that will bring the white
    death
Secretly down and choke you?
                              There is a power
Gathering in the land—O once again
Revengeful tribes of crushed American men
Are marching to the council ground, the drums
Boom all night in the valleys. If you delay
Too long in finding that again the land
Has taken right between its hands, to build it
With new vision and new will, in the old
Tried American way of beating out
Its own clear destiny, it will not matter
If you wait in high passes, eagle guarded,
Or by tall plains where the thin trail runs up
Clean to the sky, to stop that march. It will
Trample you down, leave not even your bones
As a white memorial of another death

[53]

BREAK THE HEART'S ANGER

On which America rises.
                    Let your mind
Be lithe as an Indian girl, to bend in a new
Rhythm when it hears a newer music.

Gold has been struck again, lying under
The sun's full glitter in the river bed,
Scooped up in handfuls. There is another rush
Coming. Will you be first? It is a thousand
Miles of hot wind and little water, dust
Cracking the eyes, trail blown over behind you,
Flour a dollar a pound.
                    But it is a different
Gold from any you have seen. It is the bright
Durable metal of new men, beaten out
Into the image of our land with the hard
Hammers of a new hope.
                    There is a man
In San Quentin of the lofty walls
Who, for as long as he may live, or till
His name no longer on the tongues of men
Leaves a bitter taste, will be a shame to you,
The memorial symbol of your heart's betrayal
By all the innumerable powers of greed
That shaped your living—O Tom Mooney, now
It will not be long before the wandering world
Turns in its orbit to the appointed doom
From which it will rise up and twist its life,
And yours, and all men's who so long defied it
With their own conviction of a human truth,
Into the form of its new destiny,

CALIFORNIA

And you will know that like immortal rain
You have fallen but to let another spirit
In another shape and with a different voice
Rise from the nourished earth.
                      I have heard
In drunken San Pedro with the sailors mobbing
The myriad-funneled harbor, in the valleys
That bend their heat-seared length between the
    ocean
And the Tuolumne big trees, in the cobbled
Hills of Chinatown, the mumbled words
That are the indrawn breath which will be hurled
Out of the mouth in a twisted tongue of song:

  I am the common man.
  I have sat down and wept
  Where never water ran,
  Known the Hagar tears
  For the thirsting boy, have crept
  Under my shadow to flee
  The cry of mocking years
  Chanted out of the sea.

  But never have I known
  A deeper grief by a deep
  Ocean than here where the blown
  Men of the wild foam creep
  Over the clutching sand,
  Over the gray, gull-flown
  Beaches where the sleep
  Of granite drags them down
  To die with a little gasp.

BREAK THE HEART'S ANGER

For here at the utter end
Of a country, where the clasp
Of earth fails and it falls
Into the ocean's bend
Under the hollow walls
Of the piled water, there
Is another end, the doomed
End of a nation's dream,
Here at the land's edge where
The rich soil had bloomed
The tall flower of a day
When the common man should take
Rock and sea and clay
Between his hands and make
The tower of a new day
On the old earth, to wake
From its roof, with a cry and a light,
In all common men the sight
Of a newer world where they
Would be the living heart.

That world has fallen apart.

Yet neither give up, nor pray
With lean despair on your tongues
That the old order stay.

California, rise
With mountain air in your lungs
And mountain light in your eyes.

Take with new strength the new
Way out, O follow again

CALIFORNIA

The long American trail
That wanders and winds in your blood.
Another vision of men
Roams the land and will fail
Only if you give up
And drink again the blind,
Drugged, forgetful cup
Of smugness and the old pride
That looks forever behind
To the worn-out days that hide
The bitter now and your fate.
Will your stuffed ears never find
What the empty bellies cried?
Listen and act, or hate
Will call its curse over you
Who heard that cry and tried
To follow the eager new
In another life—too late.

But go on now, while the track
In the early morning dew
Is clear and fresh and black
And you see on the Fresno plain
Far off the running pack.
Follow through wheat and clover
Before the wind and the rain
Cover the footprints over.

Follow, to find again
The continent's old quest
For a way that will shape the land

BREAK THE HEART'S ANGER

To the fury and form of its men,
Till you carry in your breast
A hope, a song and a light,
And the world will lift its hand
Pointing to you and crying,
There it is always west,
Where life is strong, and dying
Is a little pause and rest
At the ultimate clean height
After long climb and flying—
Return to earth after flight.

Eze Village, France

NEW YORK

☆

☆

CITY OF LEAN, hard planes climbing flat
Out of deep granite, pure geometry
Of the unbending line and the squared angle,
Riveted steel and piled rock carved in the wind,
Topped with the bird flight and the lost bird cry
But with no human voice—you are the last
Frenzied act of the mad age that built you
To be its unfulfilled and boasting pride
That, with the juggled bonus and the bonds
At eight per cent, drove it to your creation
Out of a life that schemed and stole and ran
All day and night, fretting its nerves away
Till the jitters and the D.T.s got it. Age
Magnificent of energy, but doomed
Deeper than death.

          City of tall spears hurled
Through the torn side of the hung sky.

                     At night
Your innumerable windows burn with flame
Till the long shafts take on a life and bend
In a slow motion—slim girls beating out
The intricate dance of recreated steel.

And you, white tower of the gleaming rock,
Long crystal cunningly carved out with rooms,

[61]

BREAK THE HEART'S ANGER

Pure lift of line, Woolworth Building, you
Are now the ultimate American thing—
New world cathedral, built and dedicated
Not unto God, but to the act of living,
With the innumerable dimes and nickels
Of a nation buried in your corner stone.

Chapel of business and the modern man
Where every dawn and evening the hundreds
Of daily pilgrims cross themselves before
Time-clock altars to help His Work—extra
Dividends declared for the directors.

You made a pocket piece of eternity,
A good luck coin—*We Trust in God, All Others
Pay Cash*, on one side, *E Pluribus Unum*
On the other, meaning, one takes from many
Wealth for a thousand men, to clink and jangle
With pool slugs and buffalo nickels.

                                 City
Of immigrant hope and quickly found despair.
In sight of Brooklyn Bridge more languages
Are spoken than from London to Leningrad.
The kids can take it, toughs, lean scavengers
On the garbage pail end of a nation's life, hard-
    boiled
Little bastards talking the ganster lingo
Of American streets, the crude and life-rich words
Born in the morning, dead by night. But the old
Who came with the bundle and the father speech
Cringe in the stinking tenement air and go

To the little shops where food of their own land
Can be had with the old names, theirs is the bitter
Finding out that it is hard to die
In a strange tongue, and that pain is not pain
Save when it comes in speech cried out when a child
For a cut hand, or a tooth.

                         You great pawnshop,
The golden sign of three balls hanging out,
The sun and moon and evening star, thinking
Some down-and-outer needing quick cash had
    slung
The limp earth over your counter, saying, Ike
What'll you give me? Look, it's almost new,
Hardly worn at all. There's a few spots here
You can rub out with a little naphtha. Nope,
Not enough. Make it two bucks and it's yours.
O.K. I'll be seein' yu, Ike. You hung the earth
With a few old guns, a banjo, a rack of pants
In the window, thinking it was yours to sell,
To haggle the price, and if it gathered dust
Mark it down for a quick turnover, or hold
A knockdown, drag-out auction—Step right up,
Laadeeez an Gennelmunn (crash of the gavel).
    What
Am I offered for this fine article, the earth?
What'll you give? What'll you give? Don't be
    bashful.
I'm offered fifty, who'll make it fifty-five?
Thank you. Do I hear sixty? Fifty-five
Bid, who'll give me sixty? Going, going,
All in, all done? It's your last chance at the earth.

[63]

BREAK THE HEART'S ANGER

Gooing, goooiing. Gone (gavel) to the man
In the derby hat. Take it away.

                              You Harlem
Nigger with malaria in his bones
Chattering your life out while the crooning
Medicine men catching the fever's pulse
With the log tom-tom, try to drag it down
With a slowed drumbeat.

                    Upper East Side Germans
On the front steps at evening with a pipe
And a mug of beer. Wheat-haired Finns chanting
The gaunt, strong poetry of loved Suomi,
The deep lakes and the snow. Firecracker
Chinks with laundries and the Mott Street dives
For the snow-dips and the cokes. American
Jerusalem, spread from Brooklyn Bridge
To the Bronx, marching tribes of Israelites
Swarming the Promised Land where the grapes
    brought back
Were big and the water sweet, race of the double
Vision, dreaming either of God or gold—
You Kike Spinoza, Sheeny Christ, your shops
Line Union Square like the worn inside of a glove,
Open one morning with a band and flowers
For the ladies, closed up next day with a sale,
Ol' clo'esmen of America, your homes
In the East River slums or Fifth Avenue
Of the glittering fronts.

                    Little Wall Street running
From church to river, where the nation's wealth

NEW YORK

Is gambled over and over, won and lost
Day after day, but whether they win or lose
There is always the quiet land waiting to take them
Under and mock them with its living gold,
The deep autumnal crops of wheat and corn,
The land that makes their frenzy seem a child's
Crying for candy after meals.
                              Island
Shored with the wandering water, by the gulls
Bounded—O Indian necklace of white shells,
Perpetually call to that city's mind
That it is builded on the earth, and all
The piled-up mockery of chambered steel
Lives in the earth's broad hand, but if its towers
Too long forget the million featured men
Who are that earth's lean instrument, the hand
Will clench and break them.

                    Now I have felt
Those fingers tighten.
                         Do you forget a great
Gray-bearded man who walked your streets once
        singing,
I love you, Manhattan, and your men, barbaric
Land, for you I make barbaric song?
He would despise the mean way of your life,
Proud of your pine-straight, wind-defying buildings
But sad for the beaten lives that fill them, for
Your millionaire churches, thieving the Old World
        Gothic,
God's gilt-edged blessings sold at six per cent,

BREAK THE HEART'S ANGER

Where the poor stink too much for the nose of
    Christ,
Jesus of the watered stock, his holy writ
The juggled balance sheet, sad that you
Have hung out on the line like dirty shirts
The old American hopes that were his song.
You are not worthy now of song, our tongues
Twist and the roped words tie them if we speak
Even curses to you. But you do not hear
In your childhood game of pitching golden pennies
At a heel-scratched line.

                    You have run your life
Away, a lost and mad dog slavering
White at the jaws, nose to the ground and panting,
Deaf to whistles and cries or your heart's breaking.
Either you find the way that you must go
Or they'll take you out in the alley—it won't be
The easy dying, chloroform mask, done
In a breath, heavy and sweet, but the tearing
    bullet
Through the taut brain, you on the flopping
    ground,
Numb feet jerking.

                Wipe that Mona Lisa
Grin off your mug, we can see behind it
The yellow mind, afraid to lose its bonds,
Its shares in the bank. Lincoln said you could fool
Some of the people all the time, and all
The people some of the time, but that you can't
Fool all the people all the time. And now
You've had your rake-off long enough, the fools

[66]

Have been put wise. You can't load the dice
And forever get away with it. They've seen
The hidden fifth ace up your sleeve.

                   Come clean
Or they'll take it out of your hide.

                    They're on to you,
Your hard-luck story, from now it's going to be
Tougher than hell to mooch a cup of Java
Or a free smoke. You've pulled the elbow of God
Once too often, scraping your feet and whining,
Brother, can you spare a dime?

                   You tried
To buy, because you wanted to show the world
You were a big shot—And there's plenty more
Where that came from, it's a long way to the toe
Of this old sock, and it's full of iron men—
A continent on margin, but the market
Jumped too fast that time, you were caught short
And couldn't raise collateral, even
Throwing in your pants. And now at last you're
    broke,
Bankrupt, every nickel attached. You're only
A down-at-the-heels, second-rater, trying
To dodge your creditors.

               I have seen
The tall day come at evening and rest
Its tired head on the white throat of those towers
Until it slept and the long arms pulled night
Out of their pockets and spread it over the eyes,
Singing the deep throat songs of hanging steel
That arrowed up and circled over the town

[67]

BREAK THE HEART'S ANGER

Like lake-desirous ducks, until the dawn
Climbed from a subway bench and stumbled down
Broadway to the Battery.

                           I've seen
The worn men come in twilight with their bones
Weary for the flesh they carried, bent
Under the unbearable weight of life
Heavy with emptiness, and stand in line
For a bowl of soup, a hunk of bread. Their shuffling
Feet grind under them at every step
The tragic heart of you, New York. That line
Runs up the Hudson, through the Mohawk Valley,
Across the prairie, over the Tahoe Pass,
Down to Frisco. It is a lariat
Coiled around the neck of America
With the hard knot at your throat. Don't you
    know
You're standing on your coffin, that it looks
Like a backwoods necktie party? With a shout
Some morning—O.K., Jimmie, let 'er go—
They'll drive the wagon off and leave you dangling
For the unemployed to steal your clothes.

                              You are,
New York, the living, by your self-doomed image
Of the immeasurable cruelty
Of men to man, of man darkly become
By the wild chemistry of modern living
No longer human, but society,
With little pig eyes turned in upon itself,
Rimmed with red for any who dare touch it,
Blind to the individual, brooding

[68]

NEW YORK

In a boar-tusked corner of its pen, eager
To fight at the common slop trough till its feet
Plunge in the garbage.
                              While the single heart
Breaks with a tiny cry.

                              Hard Manhattan
Face with twitching jaws and a loud mouth,
Staring with nervous eyes over the harbor
Where ships float in on the tide like swimming rats,
Do you look for help or a way beyond the water?
Have you forgotten that you once turned back
The lands at the Atlantic edge and cried,
I'm through, from now on it's myself?
                                        Then look
Westward, to the Jersey shore, find in
Yourself, if you can, your own peculiar way
That will again make the poor, common man
The end and spirit of your life. But know
That over Europe runs a clanging word
That echoes here, and men will take it up
And shout it east and west till the whole land
Rings with its iron sound, and they will give it
The accent of America.
                              You skirt,
Statue of Liberty, hurl down your torch
Till the waves blind it. Hide your face. Give up
The hypocrisy of thinking that you are
The symbol of an old American right.
You are its living ghost, a travesty
Of the bare act of living. Now ten million

BREAK THE HEART'S ANGER

Jobless men defy you. If you have
Tears behind those bronze, gull-haunted eyes
Weep them, take their comfort, or else crumble
Into the bay, for liberty is now
Like the sea's motion by the squat moon driven
To break on the grinding beaches of the world
And run down broken to the flung tide's doom.

Here is our newest statue of liberty—
Old lady with a box of Pippin apples
At a nickel a throw, in upper Times Square, wait
But a little longer for a customer.
Patience. The change is coming. Only today
It walked in Union Square an hour.
                                        Grim
City, despair riding the radio waves
Into every heart, as when in the London nights
Of plague they drove carts down the deadly streets
Crying, Bring out your dead, Bring out your dead,
I'll come with a Wop pushcart in the worn night
Crying, Bring out your dreams, Bring out your
        dreams.

But there is another and a newer dream
Loose in the land like a Maine deer driven down
To the village by deep snow. It is a live,
Hot-blooded, running thing with a proud head
Lifted over the curved-wind neck, and eyes
Deep with the sight of what they have not seen.

Now I have heard the buck through the dark timber
Bugle his time long call.

NEW YORK

                    And heard, New York,
In the voices of your men on Bowling Green
A huddling, half-known chanting and a shout
That barely has the body of a word
And yet is the eternal human cry
That comes when in their violated hearts
Men know that it is better to rise up
And die in the gutter, fighting to bring in
A shape and meaning to their lives, than go
On and on with a life whose every breath
Mocks the blood-gasping and defeated lungs
That suck it in.
                    And I have heard that shout
Boom in the streets until the frayed tongue split:

Down vertical planes of light
Hung with hurtled steel
Our heart's faith and the sight
Of our eyes plunge and reel.
Here at the greatest height
Of proud built tower and wall
Where our hopes from the street
Should rise over the tall
Hundred stories, they beat
Against piled rock and fall
Lower and deeper than all.

For they have made of the city—
The hands of power that can
Blind the eyes to pity—
A clip-joint, one flight down,

BREAK THE HEART'S ANGER

With knockout drops they've drugged
The common American man
Lost in the streets of that town;
With brass knucks they have slugged
And beaten that man cold,
Tied him and robbed and gone
Through his pockets, have rolled
His little cash, and at dawn
Out in the street they've thrown him
In the gray gutter, there
Till the bulls come, to lie—
No one will say he's known him
Well, they'll stand and swear
It's queer that he should die
In that same city where
He lived with an old friend,
And that it's tough and sad
He should have such an end,
He, the hard worker, glad
For a job, the chance to save
A bit for a rainy day.

The town will buy his grave.
It is very kind that way.

Take a slant some time
At faces that turn gray
In subway exits, stay
Once in a flophouse, dime
A bed, and you will see
You've made from the strange way

NEW YORK

Of our American life
A racket that will be
A hard and hungry knife
Leaned on your throat, until
You know in mind and heart
The vision and the will
To make each man a part
Intrinsic to the whole
In the creative scheme
Of a nation made at last
To the clear shape of its soul,
And men will find their dream
Of the country made one vast
Union of shop and land,
Factory and town
Formed to the good of all
Its living men, the planned
Hope of new life come down
From the vague sky, the tall
Heights of dream, to stand
Full and proud in its hand.

Now, Manhattan, take
The lead again and let
The deep tide lift and break
First on you. O set
Your hungry face against
The West that is to be—
Not acres to be fenced
But a new history.
No more the pioneer,

BREAK THE HEART'S ANGER

The ax, the covered wagon,
The wolf, the hunted deer,
The drained corn-whisky flagon.
Put back the too long treasured
Symbols of your youth
For the tough, bread-line measured
Fact of a hard truth—
That now the old life ends
With the old hope, that now
The earth is torn and bends
Beneath a newer plow:
A cabin not the sign
Of our American fate,
But a steel sinewed line
Of the hard Empire State.

Now, New York, you great
Water fowl, arise
From the deep island grass
Where all day long your eyes
Watch the tall funnels pass.
Climb from the hollow, keel-
Torn harbor, O shy bird,
Gull, or migrant teal,
At the quick call of a word.
Rise from the waters where
You now have lain too long,
Fly the wing-wandered air
With hard, beak-bitten song.
And take your men along,
The lean, life-fated men,

NEW YORK

You must avenge their wrong
Before you fly again.
Rise up to your new birth
And let your life doom be
Not one day more an earth,
But a wind, destiny.

London

ATLANTIC PASSAGE—EAST

THE GOLDEN BAT of day on western wings
Breaks the Atlantic sky and hides the land
Under its yellow shadow. When it moves
Beyond the Catskills let us turn our heads
To the gray mist and morning where it came
And on the darkened pathway of its flight
Plunge to the east, from Coney Island out
To Cornwall and that other continent,
That little head on the huge bulk of Asia
Rolling loose.

        There must all wisdom move
Deep and certain in the minds of men
As the long history that through those lands
Wandered on the minnesinger's feet
Or poured down coldly like remorseless rain.
There, surely, can be no hard tragedy
Like our dreams broken underneath our eyes.
Will we not find that all the waste, the wonder
Of our disintegrated life, despair
Stuck in our ribs, are but a child's confusion
Gone with his growing?

        America at noon
Stands in its shirt sleeves and with open throat
Shadowless in light, while Europe walks
With the black shadow of its centuries

BREAK THE HEART'S ANGER

Trailing behind it like an open grave
Waiting its death. But lean in front of us
The glittering blind shadow of the future
Runs from our eyes out to eternity.
We have looked too long against the fiery west,
Always our face has watched a falling sun.
Now let us go where the thin edge of dawn
Breaks night and earth apart.

                        O there it lies,
The enormous cross of Europe, on it nailed
The shape of Western man, the weary head
Of Spain drooping on one side, the arms
Of Italy and England flung out far,
The limp feet trailing off into the Urals,
The jagged spear of war against his side,
The west wind's bitter sponge upon his mouth.

It is again like that old man of Greece
Who stood without regret and from the lips
Of stupid men heard his doom mumbled out—
When the ship comes from Delos you will die.

Now from the cliff its purple sails are seen.

But there are words upon his tongue, perhaps
He can tell many of the mysteries:
The meaning of a rat's feet in the dust,
The agony that travails in a seed
And sends the white roots down, the green stalk up,
The touch of loving on the mind, the strange
Mystery of lifting up a hand,

[80]

ATLANTIC PASSAGE—EAST

Why men starve for having too much food,
Or why the mountains of the world are marching
And with them the world's men, their booted feet
Making a tiny tramp against the moon,
Hiding almost the whisper of that voice:

Never through book,
Blooded creature—
That backward look
Into the future—
The lean eye took
Tomorrow's feature.

But you must stare
Into men's eyes
Until your hair
Stands up like cries
Seeing at last
And bitterly
All that has passed
And is to be.

So you will take
The hawk's hard lean
On the wind and break
The light between
Your hands and build
With your long, curled
Fingers the skilled
Shape of a world.

[81]

BREAK THE HEART'S ANGER

There you will find
That your feet follow
Never the blind
Roots of the willow
But the hard mind,
The heart's dark hollow.

Walchsee, Tirol

ENGLAND

☆

Beyond the scilly isles, the Lizard light,
Flashes the Eddystone before that harbor
Where long ago the little ships went out
And headed west, for no remembered port,
Where no reef-hidden channel had been charted,
Where no dry dock lay waiting for repairs,
Where the dark hills behind the hollow beach
Held only emptiness, the arrowed death,
Trees unfamiliar and no ax-blazed paths
River to river where the fords were known.

Here from Plymouth have the Devon sailors
Driven the massive, moon-loud tides of earth,
Rounded the capes, weathered the gales, defied
The sleety mast, to Dartmoor cottages
Brought the coiled coral and the whale harpoon.
The full reversal of America
Is here, the gray and gulf-warmed edge of Europe.
Here is the trapdoor of a continent,
Lift up the island, peer at the enormous
Cellar walled with France and Russia, loud
With the green ocean water.
                              Here that voyage,
First with women to the homeless West,
Weighed the lean anchor and from sight of hills
Friendly with all the man-worn earth of England

BREAK THE HEART'S ANGER

Sailed to the friendless land. Now here come back
After three hundred years, to the old house
Where children played before they went away
Leaving the marbles in a colored sack,
The secret caves, the bird eggs blown and strung,
The riddles cried for counting out, the rimes
For skipping rope, the nicknames, all the cryptic
Symbols carved on fences, made with fingers.
Now the return of blood to parent heart
Though changed in color by an ocean width,
Doomed with a faster pulse, and yet a blood
That, from all the many-hearted world
Gathered in one terrific artery
Mixed irretrievably, cannot flow back
Into the single, elder vein, but throbs
Uneasily like any bruise.
                              Yet here
Begin the old, ancestral countries, here
Surely can we find all certitude,
All friendliness to men, all gentleness
To women, all the peace experience
Gives to those who in the human way
Have watched the centuries pile up like leaves
In a windy corner of their lives and taken
A human wisdom. Here indeed must be
No deep betrayal of a nation's dreams,
Nor anything like the doomed bitterness
In our American defeat of living
Haunt the time-hallowed mind.
                              By Roman Road,
Along the Fosse Way or the Watling Street,

ENGLAND

Through London by-pass or through Berkshire
    lane,
To Great North Road, beyond the Roman Wall,
With hope and confidence and curious eyes
Let us go on into the English land
To lift our fingers up and touch its life.

So ancient in the earth, your stream beds filled
With the chipped pottery of many peoples,
Hills ringed with Saxon camps, with the deep forts
Held for a night against the howling Picts,
So edged with murmuring whiteness mournfully
Out of the green tide moving, so with glory
Filled, your history, of daring men,
Greatest of all in song, their natural speech,
So blessed with men whose voice was that of birds,
Winged with music.
               What have you become?

In every port your ships rot and your sailors
Loaf on the docks, in London every street
Is black with beggars and through all the land
Are worse than beggars, men whom you have
    bought
With a few shillings threatened from the rich,
Enough so they will not die, and not enough
To give them strength for dreaming, for demanding
Their simple right as Englishmen, that right
Of liberty in living you have bragged
Was the great English good, they have not even
The humble right to work, to hold a job,

BREAK THE HEART'S ANGER

To keep a decent house, to feed their children
Honest food when they are fever eyed
With the lingering despair of malnutrition,
While all your smug and money-padded folk
Think it a little sad the lower classes
Have a rough time, and yet are not their griefs
Only the customary tears of things?

Tortured with faces, O Trafalgar Square,
The white, lean faces twisted with their living,
Innumerably featured, frail bone molded,
Nailed with beaten eyes to the bowed skull,
Pallid with rotten air and little sun,
Here are your ghosts, come before they die
To haunt you, hollow symbol of their grave.
They are more ghostly, more remote from living
Than, in this gallery, the painted heads
Staring through canvas like a crack of time
Into the present—faces hard with pain,
Bloated with pride, intolerant with ruling,
Gentle with loving—but the eyes, the eyes,
Penny flat, deeper than all lost space,
Bright with the memory of little things
Held in the inscape of the homesick mind,
Blinded with light, bitter with the wind,
Wild with the sight of all worn human moving
Through the hand incredible, ear unbelieving,
Body hungry and mind-maddened world
Where driven men and women while their death
Cries in their lungs and batters in their blood
Throng, haunt and beat the intolerable earth

ENGLAND

To find the unbuilt home that is no where
Save in the brain-broad country of themselves.

Even the dead are shamed by your defeat.

Have you not seen them, gathered at street corners
All day long, pale with hopelessness,
Watching the curb for cigarette butts, waiting
For that vague job they know will never come?
They are the germs, clustered in your joints,
That one night, suddenly, before you've time
To call the guards or blow the air-raid sirens
Will swarm your blood stream, clog your arteries,
Torture the tongue, burn the eyes black with fever,
And by dawn leave you stretched on the cold
        ground
Riddled with that disease which comes to nations
From deep in the musty marrow of their bones
When they forget that even the dead moon
Moves through phases, that they live in time
Which by no iron rivet, white with fire,
Hammered with steam drill, may for long be
        welded
Taut on the girder of eternity.

Desert doomed, Elisha land, waiting
For the dark ravens that will never come.

The shafts unworked, the coal untouched in seams
While many shiver and the finger tips
Of children whiten. Factories grow old

BREAK THE HEART'S ANGER

Not with wear but by the subtle rot,
The unimaginable, grim decay
Of idleness in the same way your mind
Under the vague attrition of so many
Centuries of muddling through, will crumble
Into a pinch of dust and blow away
Never knowing that a land at times
Must move more quickly and must act more
    largely
Than an hour or two of cricket after tea.

Have you forgotten dreaming men in whom
The names of all your island counties rang
With a clear bell tone over the bent hills
Making them glad to plow your fields and talk
An English language to an English wind?

Lear-like, you ripped your eyes out, to complain
That all the world was dark and dizzy height
Down which you fell forever with a cry
Of self-willed terror, stopped your ears, cut off
Your hands so you could neither hear nor touch
And went thus through your nerveless private
    world
Without the sense of movement or of light
Or apprehension of the human fact—
Stay there in darkness if you will, but once
Regain sight, sound and touch and you will know
The old remorseless cry of human pain
Too long strangled in the purple throat
That will not take the shape of any word

ENGLAND

But with a meaning you will understand,
The long unuttered shouting of your doom,
The clear decision of intent, your death.
And you will see that most unbearable
Of all the sunlit or the moonlit forms
Taken by the reflected light of things,
The massive, muttering image of the poor,
The thumbs of living thrust deep in their neck
Till the breath choke, all space upon them leaning
Its ponderous, terrific weight until
The human shape and all the lines of person
Grope and gather to a living face
With the innumerable characters
Of men and women furiously cut
Into the fluent skin and the warped bone,
Domed on the arched forehead with despair.

You will touch with trembling hands that face
And draw them back burned to the moldy marrow.

And now you shout for Jubilee, for boasting
Of twenty-five long years of misery,
Chanting the praises of a reign that twice
Damned itself: once with the bloodiest war
That the world's eyes, though used to massacres,
The legion slaughters that have always written
The chronicles of nations in that red,
Lost, beating fluid, ever have endured—
To keep your markets and to capture more.
Once when those markets failed, and all for want
Of little things had in too great abundance

[91]

BREAK THE HEART'S ANGER

Your men must walk the streets and turn to home,
Empty pocket, empty heart, with hands
Empty of work, and now you hold an empty
Pomp before them, cruel mockery
Of all the joy they cannot feel.
                         What cause
Have these poor men for any jubilation,
Or that dead million whom you have betrayed?
These living and those ghosts despise, defy
And will destroy you, O Narcissus people,
Staring in the waters at your own face,
Although that water be the mingled oceans
And you wave over it the mighty flag
Of a pound note, the shore you lean will crumble
And hurl you downward till that water drown
Your last mad crying, and you will be buried
Wrapped in that sea-colored flag.

                         How much
Longer, shivering at the approach
Of the inevitable change of time,
The hour of movement, will you try to wear
History like a cloak against the cold?

Hamlet land, doomed by your indecision
(A cough behind the arras, an old man murdered,
A mother poisoned and an uncle stabbed),
Delay, delay, lunge not while he is praying,
Wait for a darker time or till the ghost
Again reprove you. Listen all day long
To those who mumble twistedly of truth.

[92]

ENGLAND

Let the mind act but never the hard hand.
Consider justly every side and never
Apprehend the whole. Mimic madness
Till the loved one go wild and wander singing
To the willow death with all her loosened hair.
Handle the skull, jab a cruel finger through
The blinded sockets, turn (Alas, poor Yorick)
Away, and not admit it is your own.
Resolve your living only as abeyance
Out of the ultimate fear, of a self death.
Defer, postpone, retract, prolong, until
The pitiless old powers of the world
Bend the clean light of time and shape from it
The inexorable image of yourself
To throw it in your frightened staring eyes
Till you know bitterly what must be done
And with a courage sucked from desperation
Accept the duel, take up the sword and fight
With all the valor of the end of things
To the last flutter of the wounded wrist
When not one is left living and you die
While the loud world is pounding at your door
To carry you away with muffled drums—
A firmer sound than ever your own speaking.

There was an old man, jobless, with no dole,
Walking down a lane by Beachy Head.
Over him one singing lark, and under,
The long Atlantic beaches, coldly booming.
I heard him talking through the bitter wind:

BREAK THE HEART'S ANGER

No more, frail bird, fly
The enormous light,
Nor break the sky
In two with flight.
Turn to me here. No more
Flutter and fall nor beat
Tired wings over the land,
Over the bare shore,
Fold them, clutch feet,
Light on my hand.

You are one part
Of life that will
The human heart
Never kill
For the doomed power
To take and hold
One quick hour
A weight of gold.
Now where you flew
Take me, being
No less than you,
Seed-hungry bird,
Tired, wind fleeing.
I with word
And you with song
Cry all day long
We are not heard.

And now you, strong
Earth-broad sea,

ENGLAND

Lean on the land
One bent knee.
With quiet hand
I touch and know you.
Let wind throw you
Over me,
Drag me down
To that abyss
Where all men drown
And the shark fins hiss.
From Beachy Head
Were the ashes thrown
Of Friedrich Engels,
Now are they fled
To all the beaches,
The stony shingles
Where England reaches
Its line of coast.
I would not fear
With that sea battered
Driven ghost
To be, to hear
The final sound
Of my lungs shattered.

Underground
Is peace with him
Gentler, less blind,
Than on this rim
Of troubled earth
Where our own kind

BREAK THE HEART'S ANGER

Hunger from birth
And their hands touch
Only dearth
So that a few
May have too much.

From this high ledge
Of the lean world
Where you were hurled
Into the blue
Sea, to you
From this clean edge
Of time I call,
O deep tide curled.
The lark that flew
And I that fall
Have more than we alone can do.

From the intolerant dark tides of ocean
Lift up your arms that were to living men
Forever open and forever kind,
With that wild water mingled utterly
Bend them around the shores of this doomed land,
Gray gull squatting on the ship fouled waves
Hunting the buoyant sewage of the earth,
And pull it down into the choking deeps
From Land's End up to Tilbury and north
To Inverness, till Snowdon and the Welsh
Mountains huddle where the fish defile them
Maddened beneath that myriad green light,
Blinding the eyes of sheep and all those men

ENGLAND

Who will not stand in line for any dole
In that long coral death, nor ever take
The enormous cold of winter on their bones,
Till the defiant waters wander free
And clean from Cherbourg to America.

Butcombe Court, Somerset

GERMANY

☆

GIVE CASTOR OIL to Goethe, let him grovel
At the feet of kultur experts with the lash
Tearing his back and all the jibbering
Travesties of thinking, feeling men
Jeering and kicking him with boots until
He sees the northern, pure and absolute
Inspiration of the human mood
Deep in the earth and troubled in the mind
As a hooked symbol that the children use
For lucky pieces.
                    Shall the world then be
A huge swastika glaring into space,
Whirling, burning, shouting to the stars
The proud defiance of stupidity?
Let the hooked crosses burn above the mountains,
There in the great snows and the mournful pines,
But will you never learn that one bright fire
In any curious and tangled form
Blazing along a hill, can never guide
A continent, a nation or all men.
A country fails unless the light to lead
Its men is a clear flame held in the eyes
Till all you look upon is burned and men
Know you have seen the ultimate straight way
Into the crooked future. Keep too long

BREAK THE HEART'S ANGER

That bent cross for the image of your life,
That cross on which you crucified so many
Christs caught in that gigantic garden,
The cruel Gethsemane of the machine,
Betrayed by the doomed Judas kiss of money,
Keep it, till like a stigma it becomes
Furiously branded on your face
For all the world to see, and deeply carven
Like an angry birthmark in the tender skin
Of all your children.

                    Beat the Jews, forgetting
You called Spinoza God-bedrunken man,
That the poor Jewish mother, Virgin Mary,
Lives in the valleys of Bavaria
Robed in color bluer than your lakes,
That Heine, tortured on a Paris bed,
Scribbled the lieder that you sing at nights
Over a can of beer in every cellar.
You who are mingled of a hundred bloods
Despise a people's purer than your own:

Footloose folk who from a desert tent
Have wandered all the countries of the earth
Driven like leaves before the fateful wind
Of malice, greed and every jealousy,
Forever homeless and forever cursed,
You have the whole, enormous world for home.

Rulers by bludgeon and the bloody knife
Hiding beneath the hollow cry of honor
Can you not see that all your humble men

[102]

GERMANY

Wish not to leap at the bare throat of others
To steal a few scant miles of planted ground,
That they want but a little job to do,
A plate of rye bread and a mug of beer,
A brass band concert Sunday nights.

But think
How often in the nourishing, deep night
Has the gigantic wheel of sleep been broken,
The belt ripped off to writhe across the room
And strike the sleeper like a brutal dream.
The bullet in the brain before he wakes.
Kill, in one mad night of slaughter, all
Who are not with you, hound through howling
    streets
Those who believe there is another way
Of building up a lost integrity
Than selling out the workers to those men
Who hang in the greedy air of every land,
Bare-necked vultures with a golden bill,
Makers of armaments and war scares, holders
Of vested interests. Knife in the back
Those with the hopeless courage to believe
That here on earth, and with their mortal hands,
Men can take the social instruments
And with the immortal human sense create
The ultimate condition of our lives
Where every worker has the right to work,
Where no man takes too much from those who have
Too little, no man hungers, no man wants
The simple, actual demands of living,
Clothing, a house and fuel against the cold.

BREAK THE HEART'S ANGER

There was a German whom you now despise,
Revile, contemn, the one above you all
Who saw beyond the frontier and the Rhine
And knew the world as one intrinsic whole,
All simple people in all lands as one,
One the magnificent old human mood
That is the light and quality of earth.
You double cursed and driven man, Karl Marx,
Being both Jew and dreaming fool, thinking
That man would not forever exploit man,
Nor break upon the marvelous machines
The simple men whose hands are skilled to run
     them.

Of him say this: he loved his wife and children,
Was gentle, generous. He wrote of money
Having none himself. Looked clearly into things
Not without humor, once said he was glad
Not to be a follower of Marx.
Bearing the misery of all the world
Upon his mind, would not admit his own.
Quiet scholar ever quick to action,
Impractical as any child, but seeing
The recurring movement of the practical.
Writing of the perpetual ways of money
And nearly starving for the lack of it.
Crabbed, satiric, bitter, merciless
To those he hated, kind to those he loved.
Hard as a friend, but never without friends.
No man of business, no economist,
Neither philosopher, and yet somehow

GERMANY

Greater and more integral than all,
Knowing the deeply fundamented base
Of life in that which gave the means of living,
Finding the only true reality
In the idea working through the act,
And all idea yet unrealized
Groping illusion, lost, unreal existence.

Here was a man firm of integrity,
Never by persecution, threat or hunger
Moved to retraction, but to more defiance.
Prouder than those who drove and battered him
From land to land, he still was fully humble
To live by charity of friends, and through
Poverty, unhappiness and pain
Strong in the faith that finally not greed,
Not legal thievery, not privilege
For one and exploitation for ten thousand,
Not war for right to sell, will be forever
The bitter logic of our mortal living.

O while the hard, tough body, iron thewed,
Of lean reality runs through the earth
On clanging feet and with straight staring eyes,
To know, behind it, the immortal shadow
Of foredoomed future, with its eager hair,
The arms all waving and the eyes all wild,
The wavering feet silent and the face
Lit with the glimmer of the end of things,
Of all that ever here must and will be,
The intolerable glare and flame of time.

BREAK THE HEART'S ANGER

That man saw both and clearly. It is that man
You spit upon the iron of your hate.
And with that hate comes all the cursed corruption
That slits the throat of art with a dull edge,
Beats out the thinking mind's terrific light
And hurls a nation back through history
To fall down clattering darkness of the past
And grow reversely to a child again.
It is the burning of the books that breaks you,
The doomed destroying of the mind in print,
Each roaring pile down every yelling street
Is a clear semaphore that flashes out
The inevitable working of your fate.
Human thought is a more subtle fire
Than any you can build with brutal hands,
You cannot stamp it out beneath your heel,
Banish it by decree or prop it up
Against a building for the firing squad.
Drive it underground, it will flare up
Through basement floors and creep through all the
        house,
Crack earth and leap into astonished day
Or rip the night with an enormous hand.
And you who burned it once it will destroy
With an intenser and more deadly flame,
For like the desperate old power of life
That winter can delay with cold and dark
It will, when the moon changes and the sun
Crawls, on yellow feet, close to the world,
Burst through snow and rock to break the neck
Of the last north wind, batter down the great

GERMANY

Door of death and fill the hollow room
Of earth with movement, urgency and growth,
Till the walls crumble with a new creation
And the light quiver in the crying air.

You have built the scaffolding of a new state
Tied with the rotten rope of human blood,
That fiber which, however much the rain
And wind may fray it, knife can never cut.
But some clear morning it will leap and clench
The throttled throat and leave you hanging there
Till the carved timbers clatter to the ground.

March through the streets in columns where no man
Is more than a stitched number on a shirt.
Yell all night long your songs of vengeance, cry
Your little catchwords, put the troubled earth
In uniform, bright boots and epaulets,
A triple row of medals on its chest,
Brown shirt and cap and all the mockery
Of simple men, and with a shout of "Hail"
To a saluting leader who has flung
All degraded and destructive powers
Loose in the country like a plague of rats,
March it goose-stepping off through startled time
Flying the terrific flag of wind
Branded with the symbol of good luck,
That hooked cross whereon you have crucified
Not condemned Christ but a despairing nation.

I have heard those driven underground go singing:

Somerset, April, 1935

[107]

BREAK THE HEART'S ANGER

Let no longer
In time's curved run
The living linger
When is only
Glitter of gun
And cruel knife lonely
For the rib sheath.

Now is hope done,
Though under a wreath
Quick green not black
Of live-oak buried
Where no man follow
His lover tarried
For one look back,
Drowned in the sallow
Earth's torn stream,
Hard rock harried,
Deeper than dream.

It is better now
For all to wander
From auto and plow
Through clay or sand or
Loam where are
No men, and eyes
Need not bother
To watch the paid
Hands of a man
Betray another
Or be betrayed.

GERMANY

Go where is ever
The flower unblown,
At dawn is heard
No song, where never
Tree is bowed
Or winged wind flown
By any bird.

Yet are times, once
In centuries,
When the world wanes
And men must pile
Their hearts like leaves
For it to scale
A little higher
The ancient wall.

If such a time
Is here and now,
Though in the climb
Of history—against the down
Falling apart
Of one long doom—
It comes rarely,
Here is my heart.

Take it early.

Berlin

VIENNA

☆

HERE THE WORLD huddles in the lee of time.

Here Europe laughed. And then the jaw was
     broken,
The tongue torn out crying with its song.

Here there was music that the guns drowned out.
Here there was dancing till the light feet twirled
One last and marched away in the nailed boots.

Here in the doom-dark streets where all night long
There is no sound but now and then the mad
Yell of a man or whimper of a cat
Is the utter anguish of a continent.

Here is the final and degraded end
Of that proud vision of a Western man
Which centuries ago and with strong arms
Threw the dark Christian God out of its mind
And with light hands on the lean knife of reason
Carved the clear image of another age,
Long in the limb, mighty of chest width,
Quickly moving, supple in the wind,
Clean eyed, curious fingered, never quiet,

[113]

BREAK THE HEART'S ANGER

Sewn with the twitching thread of nerves,
Restless and crying with the song of blood
Under wrist and throat and in the echoing heart,
Yet groping for all that it had thrown away,
Lonelier than a dog on a cold night
Whimpering by a house for a brief warmth,
The cheerful sound of human voices talking,
The smell of clothes, the friendly human touch,
Proud of its mind and its created things,
The charts and symbols and the wild machines,
The dominance, the grip on ground, the power,
The hard defiance of mysterious earth,
But always longing, groping without end,
Lifting that mind a pale and pleading hand
Up to the healing sun of certainty.

Grim of face and myriad of thought.
Plunged so deeply in the drowning water
Of self and other men and always self.
Watching its own life loom against the windy
Sky of its hand breadth and enormous skull
Sutured with bone and with infinity
Till it crumbled downward to the brain's dark
    earth,
Wailing as the twilight whippoorwills
Watch night along the river rise and fall
Into the colossal crater of the day.
Quick noon between the dawn and evening,
Haunted height above the glaring hollow,
Writhing flame hung in its own black shadow
Between the life desire and death desire

VIENNA

Poised on the balance of conflicting mood
Till quietly and with no sound but calling
With irresistible and dreaming hand
Death shakes out her dark disheveled hair
Over his eyes and blinds him and he sees
Only the humble and magnificent
Consummation of his agony.

Here in these streets he wanders on tired feet
Over the torn earth tired of bearing him,
Walking the bitter endless night of time,
Knowing the beaten way is in the stars
That through the wild darkness he can never see.

Civilian armies in decrepit pants
Joined at a dime a day for cigarettes,
Women beggars with their empty eyes,
Their arms with children and their crying hands,
The stumbling columns of the ponderous poor
Writhing around the squares like bits of string
Driven through gutters by a heavy rain.
Death is a final act—it is not that.
Nor is it living, which is force of will.
But rather that triumphant full despair
That sees each act as its repudiation,
That finds all movement stiller than unmoving,
That deep denial of a Western man
Who never dared accept what could be taken
Into the mind and wrestled with, that whole
Resignation to reality.

BREAK THE HEART'S ANGER

That watching with worn eyes, that running out
Into the night for faces glaring there
Behind the descending dark, only to see
The blind, unblinking eyeball of the moon
Staring in marvel at a blinder earth.

Who has not, at midnight, felt the Ring
Quiver, contract and grip the city's heart,
Or seen the Danube with its biting blade
Stab the great body till it could not cry?

Here was the highest peak of Europe's living
In one old mood. Here is its lowest depth
Before the new.
           And here the new flared once—
All you who bore the guns at Karl Marx Hof,
Behind the thin walls open to the hill
From where the cannon and machine-gun fire
Came point-blank, you ratted through the sewers,
Knifed in cellars, tracked down in the mountains
Because you stretched the thin thread of your hope
From earth clean out to eternity and thought
To walk there boldly in the sun's despite.
You had belief and then they beat you down.
You saw the way and then they ripped your eyes.
You knew tomorrow as an April lark's
North returning wing one shadow breadth
Lifted into the southern sky and dropped
Before you heard its song.
                But now these words
Mock and not praise you, being actual men

[116]

Who struggled grimly in an actual world.
Yours was the gray terrific tragedy
To see the new age running in the streets
And after it the ghost of a new man,
Then suddenly to watch the stolid powers
Of yesterday and property and wealth
Take the new heart of man across their knee
And break it like a stick.
                    In your defeat
Is the certain triumph that has always come
When vision met with courage and the two
Ran through the world like man and shadow, like
Hand and its action, mind and its moving thought.
Now in the coiled corruption of our life
Where the brain shakes at what it sees in brain,
Where pride is not a strength but merely pomp,
Where calm humility is but a mask
For double arrogance, where dignity
Lies, and not deeply, in a stolid rock,
In one straight tree, but never in a man:
Yours is the pride of those who would not change
For fear or even death's complete negation
Their own conviction of a human right,
Yours the hard humility of saying
My life is little but this cause is great,
And yours the dignity of all who died
In all times for all recreated truth,
Who laid their bodies down where the bold future
Might walk into its being over them,
Who, in the world's domed darkness, could build
   up

BREAK THE HEART'S ANGER

A little fire of dedicated lives
To light the quick feet of tomorrow, dancing
Its leaping laughter on the trampled earth,
Who moved into the multitude of things
And took the bullet in the eager breast.

Below the Opera, by the Danube
Is a different, a more desperate song:

Swing, swing, Vienna feet,
Waltz hunger and pain away,
Dance till the music change and you
Glide in another day.

Put not your hand before your eye
To see how fitfully it stares,
Nor watch the others move where each
Face like a death mask glares.

You were afraid to touch the rain
Knowing it brought new growth, new start,
To hear the thunder break at night
Lest one crash burst your heart.

Have you not heard through all your streets
The final sound of your doom flying—
The wailful, gasping, hungry sound
Of little children crying.

Hold it not proudly up, but take
Between your hands your humbled head,
And hear your unborn children shrill
Calling to the dead.

Vienna

[118]

RUSSIA

HERE, AMERICA, another land
Boned like you with plunging space and blooded
With the broad arteries of pounding rivers
Beating with a swift current's pulse, has hurled
Back its head with dark, half-Eastern eyes
And flung into the clenched teeth of the world
A new, a towering and a mighty song
Hard with the howl of wind on wailing steppes,
Mournful with all the myriad Russian mind,
By a great mouth whose lips move equally
Into a snarl or to gigantic laughter
From lungs by the curved Urals hugely ribbed,
With one whole continent to ring its echo.

Through the cold hollow of all history,
In the dark cavern of all lived out time,
Into the troubled gloom of the dreamed future
Will that cry tremble in the battered air
Louder than can the world or Godwound bugles
Torn with the trumpeting of all creation
Blow the beginning or the end of things.

Here where the heavy past came lumbering
Latest into the century, where hung

BREAK THE HEART'S ANGER

The millstone of inertia on the neck
Of one vast land, where all the brutal darkness
Of unchange was a wall behind its eyes
Hiding the movement and the play of time,
Here with the shriek of the old way cut down
Without remorse, the pitiless oppressor
Murdered in the palace without pity,
Came the first light into the world's closed eyes,
The first conviction that another age
Had shuddered through the soil and ripped the air
And burst out crying to the bell-deep sun
Booming its golden echo over earth,
The first proud image of the century
Eager to run the world's long wandering roads
And shout to all men in all countries—Never
Think you have lived in the immediate
Moving of things, or watched the nervous now
Quiver before your eyes. It was the past
Whiter than blind snow fallen through your brain
Masking the restless multitude of change.
Here is the double mystery, the double
Present that is the flux of common acts
And yet the long direction, the lean power
Driving into the future a hard hand
That grips the fluent form of daily living
Into the shape and temper of tomorrow
Fashioned with fury.

                    But this land has known
Before, the explosion of all thought, the bleak
Madness of man when he has touched the earth
And found with startled hands and mourning eyes

RUSSIA

That he is human and another thing:
So Tolstoi felt the turning of the world
As God's great head swung round and round
    through time
And thought to touch it in a barren rock,
A fertile field or in his own soul's raging.
And there has never been a man who knew
Deeper than Dostoievsky the heart's anger,
That wild darkness of the driven mind
When it roams wailing in the skull's bare waste
And the eyes burn it with the fire of sight,
When the bending bones quiver like stuck nerves,
The idiot flesh snarls at all frightened thought
And for a time man is not even dream,
Not so alive, but one quick cry of pain
When the lone man in terror runs away
From his own self and in the cringing dark
Trips on his lunging shadow there and crashes
Into the body of himself. And now
Another anger roams the Russian land
With its own shadow.
                It was a grim birth.
The agony gigantic, all the limbs
Groping and twisted and the maddened mind
Purpled with pain. The inexorable wail
Tore the taut ears of the imploring world
And hung before its unbelieving face
More actual than sight. O tragic eyes
Of man that through all centuries the light
Has bruised and stroked and ripped with images
Hovered in leaves or beaten into iron,

BREAK THE HEART'S ANGER

Bladed with the keen edge of death and dark,
With the lined hunger in the forlorn face—
Always the beautiful, the brutal glimmer
Of human faces mourning or in laughter,
Carved in the granite skin softer than wax
With all the strange infinity of person—
Soft hands huddled deep in the friendly skull,
Quivering like cut fingers helplessly
At the unimaginable, fleeting touch
Of one sun ray creeping through the wind
Or one catastrophe that beats you down
With the cruel enormity of human wrong,
Poor nerve-wild fingers of the groping mind,
Will you never learn to reach far out and take
The bitter logic of reality,
To touch with all the mild skin of your pity
The mad convulsions of creating earth?

You who lift your arms and plead in horror
Against the certainty of action, you
Burned by the simple sunlight of the real,
You men of all the world who crawl away
Into the dark where you are safe from doing
What must be done, or seeing what must be seen,
You will be known as the twilight people
Who day long in the black room of your thought
Moved restlessly from chair to chair, reading
In quiet hours by artificial light
With always window curtains drawn against
The intolerable, glazing sun of hope.
Do not forget that fingers on the neck

RUSSIA

Crawl unforeseen in darkness.

                              Mountains rise
Out of the solid rock and oceans fall
Into the deep abyss, the edge of earth
And all the massive granite under it
Move and are twisted in their every shape
By that immemorial old violence
That is the way and figure of deep change.
Did not the earth plunge with terrific power
Out of the sun's torn body? Was not even
Your own beginning such a bitter birth,
America, when from Ticonderoga
To Bunker Hill and Charleston and Cowpens
The farmers, the lean, squirrel-rifle men,
Marched stragglingly like their own cowherds, men
Eager as you to plant the April corn
And take the autumn harvest in long peace,
But ready, when the inexorable iron
Of hard necessity ran through their heart
To draw it out and on the battered forge
Of their own driven but desiring lives
Beat it with ready hands into the future,
Knowing it best to take what is to be
And shape it in the humble way that men
Can fashion in one little noble part
The inevitable mood of things.

                              You proud
Scorners of deep-foundationed earth, seekers
In all the winds of heaven in all times,
Carvers in bark and searchers under stone,
Divers through water, diggers in the wind,

BREAK THE HEART'S ANGER

Lookers beneath old leaves, readers of bones,
You restless wanderers through earth, content
Only with discontent, you doomed to dream
With not the patience to accept but only
The pride to strive against and to deny
In bold defiance of the doomed to be,
Having the fateful will to challenge fate,
To lift your hands above your head when all
The brutal weight of heaven held them down
Under the straining arms, always to take
The death in struggle when to yield was living,
You givers of shape to all the vague and void,
Carpenters of the human, real creation,
Builders in the immortal ways of men:
Cromwell and all who act with the hard hands,
Robespierre and all whose power is speech,
Garibaldi and the singing thousands,
Ethan Allen and the ragged, swearing
Green Mountain boys with pine twigs in their hats,
Sitting Bull and all who said, "Our home
Is our heart, take the one, the other dies,
But kill the heart before you take the home,"
Lenin and those few—Christ perhaps and Plato—
Who took the world, a tired and sleepy child,
Into their arms and sang to it and after
Laid it down stronger and not the same child.
The world's fools and the makers of that world.

So you who saw the present and your power
On the right hand and the left hand and took

RUSSIA

The utter chance.
     What one in the world's
Catalog of men who took that world
Between their hands and left a broad thumbprint
Deep in the earth, or here a palm's thin line,
Was like this short man Lenin, long exiled,
Hunted through alleys—they had caught his
  brother,
Killed him because he had the double curse,
Youth and a tongue that spoke what the eyes
  saw—
Poor, laughed-at and a price put on his head,
The body supple in the awkward clothes,
The eyes born to sadness, the lean hands
Graceful as a girl's but the jaw hard?

There was a man in Illinois who took
His life, like Lenin, from the common folk
And gave it to a continent. He too
Came up unknown to the height of power—
In prairie train with flags and cheered by thou-
  sands,
The other in a war train, sealed and dark,
Moving with mystery behind the lines—
Though he, the rugged wrestler, would have
  towered
More than a long head above the Russian,
And no two faces more diversely featured
Have been a presence or have borne a name,
Yet each face had the same hard honesty,
The forward-looking hope beyond despair,

BREAK THE HEART'S ANGER

Both had been humble lawyers of a sort,
Both had given their heart's love to one woman—
When Lenin lived in prison one long time
He wrote Krupskaya, "Every morning come
And stand beyond the wall, for in our walk
Once around the court, through a thin slit
I can see you nearly for a second, speak
No word, but only stand and smile at me."
She was with him in poverty and pain
And would not leave him. It was strong and good.
You who call this man murderer and cruel
Think of this love. And Lincoln left his heart
Deep in a girl's grave in Illinois.
Both took the staggering and brutal weight
Of their own country's future on their eyes,
Seeing the double way ahead, and each
Bore on his back the cross of parting roads
And died there knowing that the way was taken,
Their own hands nailed. But as the blood flowed
        out
From the torn side, all quickened time flowed in
And brought with it the sight of staring men
Who through all centuries would bless them there
As the proud image of their own life walking
Darkly along that road in earth.
                                        And what
One man, Trotsky, can be named like you—
Your hard eyes hooked in men like beaks, the
        glitter
Of tense nerves piled into a fire behind them,
The nose leaned forward splitting the hard future,

[128]

RUSSIA

The mouth bitter but somehow delicate
With all the madness that was in your life,
The hair writhing from the weary head?
Take the face together, all the features,
Watch the intelligence, the steady light
Of the clear mind at work, the desperation
Of brain furiously bent with dream.
America has known a man like you
In every part and quality opposed
Of feature or of person—grave landowner,
Haughty, white-wigged Washington, knowing
His own place and his servant's—but in this
The same man: When the land of each despaired
And the tough thumbs of hate were at its throat,
Each put the dreaming straightly from his eyes
And with bare acts that are a sort of dream
Worked in the gaunt and gray reality
Till the grim work was done. You, Trotsky, built
An army out of tramps and peasants, trained
A week, with luck, and with yet greater luck
Given a uniform, a decent gun,
And with the shrewdness of a supple mind,
And all the courage of an army fighting
Back to back, so neither front could give,
Destroyed, with destitution and despair
For your munitions, those who came to break
The young land for the trembling of the old.

So you, also, with the few ragged men
Scraping the frozen blood at Valley Forge,
Felt the same presence of necessity

BREAK THE HEART'S ANGER

With all the consecration of the other,
With all the praying that he has despised,
Driving with an equal sense and patience
And men more destitute in discipline,
In uniforms, in arms, in all but courage,
The greater army back into the sea.

Let the earth give these men an equal praise
Who with the same defiance, the same dream,
Beat in the bottom girder of the tower
Raised each in his own land to a new life,
Its symbol and its being piled in one,
The rivet tempered with a human blood.
These came obscurely, with no premonition,
Into the world—no cloud that gave not rain
But burning eagles, no hound bitch that whelped
Half dog, half woman pups before a church,
No child on a street corner with a shout
Threw its thin heart into the wind and cried,
"Stare at my eyes and see immortal God,"
Till the heart cracked and in a clang of thunder
Both disappeared—and yet they left that world
No more the same but with a nobler light
Mingling with all time's moods upon that face
Where the lined skin of history is stretched
On the world's skull.
                         Nameless ones who died
Sprawling the gutters by the Winter Palace
On that November day when the great wail
Of birth, of a creating country, ran
The length of Russia—lean wolf from the steppes

RUSSIA

A thousand years starved, hounded, hunted,
    tracked
Into its hole, the tired bones bent with running,
The padded feet all splintered and the lungs
Crying with blood, the lean wolf of the people
Fanged with oppression's hate—now a new cry,
The yelp of triumph and the cold death rattle
Whose echo was the climbing room of wind
Over the earth's foundations without walls,
On that destroying and upbuilding day
When shaggy clouds like tangled hair fell down
Over the bloodshot eyeball of the sun
And on the bodies of despairing men
Was built the figure of the century,
The lean, boned skeleton that waited time
And the full hope of men to flesh it out,
To fill the heart with an insistent blood,
The nerves with sense, the mouth with taste, the
    eyes
With a whole sight.

              So Dante had his dream
Of Paradise and he, mortal, alone
With God and the bold beauty of a woman;
Being too much of fire and light compounded
He found the real a visionary fire
Save when he quarreled with nobles or his neigh-
    bor.
So Michael Angelo and shrewd Da Vinci
Found in men's bone and muscle and the face
Furious with every human mood,
Tense, troubled, singing, meditative, mild,

[131]

BREAK THE HEART'S ANGER

The face of man that is the face of madness,
But always the enormous face of God
Haunting the head and staring through the eyes
With an immortal anger.

             In that island
Stuck like an ear on the huge head of Europe
Shakespeare drank his ale and beat the table,
Took the obscene and noble human heart
Forever with him in one gentle hand
And with the understanding of all time
That moves and hovers in the lives of men
Wrote with its hot and agonizing blood
What the mouth utters but with trembling lips,
Not the firm Greek repose of the calm mind,
Though calm but after struggle and unrest,
Not peace or ecstasy of the gaunt God
Smoothing the bone-groined face with hands of
    blindness,
But the hard human look and that alone:
The simple watching of the simple earth,
The wild, the wilful and the quick to tears,
The terrified of night and the sun loving,
Twisted with too much searching after truth
Or stupid with a less than animal
Taking without question what has come,
The lips of laughter and the teeth of hate,
The lean with kindness and the fat with lust,
All forms of feeling all too bitterly
Beaten with iron into the yielding skin,
Always the conflict and the curse of will,
Man against man and woman against all,

[132]

RUSSIA

The fury of minds desiring each the same,
The struggle of the unlike for the one thing
Till the man tremble and the tight bones crack
And the one person leap against the other,
The red flame set against the yellow flame:
And that most bitter and consuming thing,
The inner snarling of that conscient voice
To which all uttered words are but the echo,
The writhing and the cry of the self-will
In the wild anger of its self-defeat.
One point poised against another point
Till the mind shudder on the balanced edge,
The teeth destroying what the hands have made,
The terrifying tension of the self
That is the strength and argument of life
And the brute cross on which the arms are bent
Wide to embrace what is their misery,
Groping toward that full agony in taking
What the hands wish with all desire of touch
To gather fiercely unto the hurt breast:

And that one ultimate sure human mood,
The curse of cruelty to all we love,
The strangling of the throat that we have soothed
Because it is too tender in our hands,
The choking of its pulse because our own
Beats with it too intensely with one beat,
The tongue declaiming what the heart denies,
The face of love, like mountain-kindled fire,
Seen moving madly only in the dark
That it must cut to make a place for living.

BREAK THE HEART'S ANGER

That deep voice talking was the cry of doom
For the long multitude of days and years
That scorned the full Greek mind and its clear light
For the piled darkness of the deity,
The groaning after God, the call to arms
Because a man had said a different thing,
The frightened dreaming that the little self
Had been created from eternity,
The one life, dreamed and shaped by the great
     Ghost
Brooding above the booming void of time
Here between the huge and lesser stars,
The suns with all the planets and their moons,
Hung on the earth to plunge with it through space
And live forever like immortal light
Hurled from the sun against the moon and then
Reflected outward to infinity.

And it was the red, ringing call to life
Of all time after him and of this age,
Our birthright and our simple way of living
That scorns the magic and the mystic stupor,
The incantation and the plea for self,
That will no more on the hard wall of God
Beat its head, nor plead with empty hands,
Nor cry in the anguish of a squeaking soul
Trapped in the rat cage of its tangled blood,
But will take up, as here between the Baltic
And the Black Sea this land has done, the clear
Fact of our living in the troubled winds,
In the lean sunlight on the livid earth,

RUSSIA

The simple truth of simple men come up
Lonely out of the travail of the dust
With none to help them but their working hands
And their own mind's immensity of thought,
With no fate more magnificent than going
Back to the maddened earth that bore them.
                                        Here
The mood and movement of the century
Live in action, prophecy and name.
A hundred years ago those two men wrote,
"A specter is haunting Europe," and today
That specter haunts the hopeless nations, not
As ghost of dread but as the act of living,
A stronger life, that is a death to them.

Here can the subtle eye look down and watch
The great feet of the world walk time away.

O Lenin, bring your iron and gentleness,
Your courage deeper than our own despair,
And with the wind for tongue cry over oceans
That through the Western world another dream
Runs on the nimble feet of light and laughter
With flaming hands and eyes of morning water
Reddened with the glare of a new day,
That the old dream was written in the blood
Of Christ, but the new in the blood of men,
That now and for the first time men can go
Their strange brief way and yet not give it over
To any other's greed or watch it break
Forever in the mighty hands of money,
That now at last a man may live with only

[135]

BREAK THE HEART'S ANGER

Two possessions—life and his right in earth,
His stake to work, and not for an abundance
Of actual things compared against his neighbors
But for a chance to live with all the fierceness
Of all the human faculties, to think
Neither of God nor gold but of the long
Movement of men thrown hugely at the sky
To drive and hover there a dreaming bird
That will between the falling cloud of time
And the hard earth of space forever fly,
The wide wings beating song from the sunlight.
That now a man may wander on bare feet
And feel the strong earth under him, the sun's
Warmth over, and with eager mouth can say,
This is my heart, this is the beating center,
The burning and inviolable core
Of that innumerably fashioned world
In moving miniature that is myself,
All oceans and the island of the land
Belong to it and to all other hearts,
And it will go back darkly under them.

Does not the chipmunk running in the grass
Have his lined hole where he may hide in fear?
But where have the world's wandering men to go?

All countries in all continents they roam
Past the rich fields that cannot feed them, past
The factories that will not hire or clothe them,
Through forests where the small gray breasts of
    birds

RUSSIA

Cry in the leaves, through cities where the lean
Gashed breasts of men cry to the stupid stones
Or to the deafer ears of other men.
Yet here a nation took the challenge up
And built through holocaust and bitter hate
Their own belief and vision of a land
Given to the common good of all,
To the creating with their humble hands
Worlds and realities by us undreamed.

O scrawl with lightning on a continent,
In the black sky the huge words hung with flame,
The song and image of the century,
The simple hope that this world has denied
Unto the human creature, this strange man,
This ecstasy of the upgathered dust
By fury fathered at the sunlight's breast,
This rabbit leaping on the frightened hills
Between two ravening hounds of temperature,
The utterance and figure of his life:
From each required as his ability,
To every man according to his need.

Come, dream of every nation made
Part of one huge nation of the world,
Of that world moving out through space and time
One sphere and mood of human dignity,
Come now into your being, from these steppes
Wander the ultimate last inch of land
Wider than air, and enter it like rain,
Move through the oceans with a whale's pride, till

BREAK THE HEART'S ANGER

You and gigantic earth together move
In the shape and body of a living man
Grinding the winds beneath your feet and striding
The light between the stars. Come then into
The little house of bone in every man
Walking on quiet feet from room to room
Lit gloomily with the gray lights of nerves
Behind the banging doors of sense, until
The arteries of every common man
Pulse with the deep power and turn of earth
Dark in veins that have the heat of mountains,
All gathered oceans and the fertile plains
Heavily weighed upon the core of rock,
And dedicated to his life and death
Goes flamingly around the father sun,
The moon around him, and with all the other
Prowling planets leaps across the heavens
One with the earth, the earth made one with him.

Cry, wild caribou of the bare steppes.
Bugle the morning red to the world's hills
Till every man find on the trampled dew
The horn foot driven in the heavy grass
Or in the valleys where the light is shy
The slim doe hoof deep in the leaf-dark earth.

Color of Mary, blue
Of heaven or from what strange eyes
Too delicate to bear
The light, O you
Wrapped round the earth like air

RUSSIA

Against the primal cold,
Another hue
Cries
With the voice of madness and of man,
Not green or purple or pale gold,
But where all colors of the spectrum ran
Over the massive head
Of earth has rolled
One flaming fury of terrific red.

So is the change of mind.
Human thought no more
Dreams upward to the blind
Blue of heaven with uplifted hands
Beating like a great door
The impenetrable wind.
It gropes the light
No more, but through all troubled lands
Wanders without shame
To clutch the good
Pulse of living, the pure human blood
More bright
With a defiant flame
Than sun and day in the noon's wildness met,
And darker yet
Than ultimate burned night.

Seek no more now in the bitter sky
But in the world, O take
The sun, or the moon, light
And try

BREAK THE HEART'S ANGER

With frantic hands to make
Your living image in the granite air
Until those blades of whiteness break.
Then stoop to earth.
Dig there
In the touchable sure dust
With patient hands and plow
The actual, until you must
Raise in the here and now
Your own life's symbol, prove again
That men
Who from the wind and rain flee
Are more than the earth's rust
In all the weathers of eternity
Scaled with a little cry from the worn crust.

Why, all other nations, have you tried
To search so low for something higher,
Or lifted up your hands when a man died
To death, not living, in your fear,
Or groped in graying ashes when the fire
Burns too fiercely for you here?

Let this land mock you in your secret room
Hidden behind the barricade
That you have made
Out of blind hopes against your certain doom.

And let a quiet stone
Rebuke you, having taken
The hard attrition of all time alone

RUSSIA

With dignity change has not shaken.
You whose starved men can only pray
With hunger-dizzy head—
Give us this day
Our daily bread.
These breathing beings who are only
The indifferent, dull earth
Turned human, lonely,
The shudder of birth
Running in dust, the shock
Of wind lunged through it and the ecstasy
Of heart given to water, nerves to rock.
They have come to be
Like lava hurled up from the fiery deep
But joined forever to its source.
O give them now a little calm and sleep
And a tough force
To living, strong
As the earth's ancient vigor, the hard will
To turn and wander, long
Through wind like willow and through moons
    like sand
As time hurls up at it the dark and light
Fists of day and night
On leaping arms, the left and the right hand.

There is no more to say.
Here men have died
To tell the way.
Did you not hear? The arrogant echo cried
Mad in the mountains all one day.

BREAK THE HEART'S ANGER

It will come back and strike you in the face
Unless you know before
It is the call
To rise up, all
Men in their own place
And batter down the door
That looms between them and the wild
Realizing the new world that comes
In the old shape of a man too long a child
Whose striding moves not with the snarl of drums
But with the firmer beat
Of the wrist's pulse. He will take the cold
From the lean ice of reason and the heat
From the emotion's flame
And with that sense of a creating world
That has no name
But instinct, intuition or the power
Of life itself, will beat
Earth until the light is curled
Back from the eyes of men for one blind hour
And their hard sight is hurled
Through split eternity all gaping wide,
Past where the sun on the tall stalk of day
Blooms like a flower,
And still
Untrampled by our eyes lost planets hide,
But turning back finds once again
Earth looming like a little hill
Against huge space, and with one last desire,
In one dark vision burned upon the brain,
Sees all mortal men

RUSSIA

Cry with the sadness of their mind until
They touch the new communal world and fill
Their hearts, hungry for pain,
With all the exaltation that this crier
After living, this earth creature,
Knows in his proud earth blood as in the rain,
And each calls out unto the freezing future,
Peace, lift up your head a little higher,
To your cold agony I will
Give you my heart, its fire
May be a lesser chill.

Walchensee, Bavaria

NOTRE DAME

☆

ALL THE SKY was in the monstrous moon
That over Paris hovered not like ghost
Or maddened spirit in the darkness fleeing
But like the city's raving, rolling head
Over its hunched neck twisted to look back
Through history and find a time its eyes
Could look upon and take a little rest
Before it changed, or when the wind of sight
Would not blow up and rip them from their
      sockets,
With all the fierceness of a man who seeks
In treacherous, night-mingled memory
What all his dreamed-out childhood never knew.
But as I walked on down the Boulevard
From Montparnasse it turned and stared ahead
Beyond tomorrow, eyes wider than arms,
The whole face burning with the blood of hope,
The ears waiting for the windy cry
That over the domed hills with tongues like gongs
Men would toll and thunder to all men,
Their voice "hunger" and their echo "earth."

I turned a corner and in half moonlight,
Half electric, saw her standing there,
Not poor but pitiful, the shoulders drooped
Into the hands, the bones thin crumpled down,

BREAK THE HEART'S ANGER

A blue cape brooding on her arms like thought.
I followed her down to the Seine, that writhing
Nerve in the city's twisted body, down
Along the quays and bridges, every one
Burdened with traffic and the limp dead weight
Of legion men and acts that over it
On tiring feet and with distracted hair
Ran into time and to finality.
Her steps were slower, slower, all the gestures
Futile in the twilight.

              So we came
To Notre Dame. Suddenly on the bridge
She knelt and prayed, the dark cloak fallen down
Like a blue flower's enormous petal blown
Over her eyes, the shy heart huddled under.
She muttered there, with the terrific weight
Of ponderous cathedral and piled night
Breaking the frail words on her mouth.

                       She lifted
Her bowed head and bent arms up to the cross,
Then with a shudder threw the cloak away
And stood there naked, the white body gleaming
More fiery than all Paris in one glow
Fiercely gathered, the indignant eyes
Screaming wild sight. Beneath that bitter stare
The whole cathedral shook and from its base
With one convulsion plunged into the sky
Hurling its towers like arms against the moon
Till the whole mass took on a life and each
Line quivered, all the moving stones cried out,
The maddened building on the crucifix

NOTRE DAME

Of the lean moon hung groping. Then her arm
Ripped through the air with white and sudden fury
And in that gaunt side hanging worn and ghostly
Tore a deep gash from which wild radiance
Flowed to the earth and ran along her arm
One crying glare, and then the great stone body
Went limp and fell, and to its ancient form
That was the shape of ruin, the life gone,
Turned dark and rigid.
                Without sound the Christ
On its hard cross tumbled to the street
And battered into fragments.
               With a shout
She ran to clutch the broken head and kiss
The stony lips and cry, "My son, my son,"
While all the mantle's blue ran through her eyes.
I started toward her and she turned on me,
The girl's face tender and the gray heart broken,
The hands clenched, wailing, "Take me now, I am
Mary, mother of Christ. You have betrayed
This God, my son. I will not bear another.
I have conceived again. It stirs in me,
But I will drown it long before it dreams.
O doomed world that will drive its one God out
And have not even faith in simple earth
From which to make a greater than itself,
My son and I deny you without end.
Now we escape from your world and your time."

The frail body that was more than living,
Light woven in a woman's form,

BREAK THE HEART'S ANGER

Leapt from the rail into the waiting river
And the two heads above the water's dark
Were for an instant lonely and aloof
With that hard dignity that is not death
But the defiance of created earth
That rose and made its life and went away.

Now the blue cloak had fled into the sky.

The walls and windows and the carven angels
Stared through darkness without power or pity
Having so long endured our lifted hands,
The prayers of our mouth, and given back
The hope of hopelessness, the scorn of silence.

Church of Francis and the hungry birds,
If divine truth is anywhere or God
Moves in the earth, they are a part of you,
Ancient body of the Christ become
Only an old tongue speaking without head.

Can you not find now in the world's despair,
The generation that is Judas-Christ
Betrayed by the bitter kiss of its own self,
A nobler symbol than a tortured man?
This is the end of you and of a world.

Here a life dies—stand in a bread line
To watch its hungry haunting ghosts come back
To hover in the place where they had lived
And watch with curious eyes the earth go by

NOTRE DAME

Under the writhing wind, and one will say
That it's a tough time now for carpenters,
Tell Christ to hang his hammer up and slouch
At some street corner with the other bums
Mooching a dime from those he died to save.

Where, in 'fourteen, was your Christian grace?
What Vatican encyclical prevented
That maddened murder not alone of men
But the world's dreaming of the common man
For centuries held in the daring heart?
And yet you gave your blessing to the guns,
Counted any soul as saved that mumbled
The name of God and shot His children down.
But it is not too strange at all, there were
So few popes bayoneted, so few bishops
Waited zero hour on the firing step
Or, in the barbed wire with the belly ripped,
Reeled, and told their beads and were content.
Yet were those men not Christ, on the huge cross
Of the world hung with the gray nails of nerves?

Now have we emptied out our pockets, probed
Deep in our hearts and groped in other eyes
To find where truth is and for what wild reason
We wander on between the earth and wind
Like autumn insects in a willow, waiting
The winter cold and boring time away
Between the outer bark and the hard grain.
We are of the earth and here perpetually
With every drop of water, crust of bread,

BREAK THE HEART'S ANGER

Take its inviolable sacrament.
Yet who can lead us, who will gather up,
Not with a little pity but great pride,
The lean, bone-angled body of a man
In tender arms and hold it to the sun
And say, This is your child, give it the warmth
Of life and the four seasons varied cloaks
And two clear fires of light to be its eyes.
Or hold him to the midnight moon and say,
This is your ghost, watch over him in sleep.
If anyone, across the desert driven
By sandstorm or a God's wrath, think to guide
Our hearts through living or the world through
     time,
Let him know that when the people thirst
And cry with blackened tongues, that if he take
The immortal rod, whether it be of sunlight
Or but his finger's bone and nerve, and touch
The rock of earth, it will flow human blood.
That while the idiot now is at our hearts
And gibbering kneels upon our broken breast
Laughter is the death cry in our throats.

Lenin, we cry to you beyond the world,
But there are heavy hands upon our mouths.

Here is my hand, bent like your shepherd's staff,
To lead you, Jesus of the thorn-caught lamb,
Through all the rocky darkness of the waste
That is the brutal country of my mind
Where the lean wolves of my desiring thought

NOTRE DAME

Circle and near, with the white howl of fangs,
Closer and closer to my tiring eyes.

Do you not know, church builded on a rock,
That even stone collapses under rain,
The tear of fingers and the claw of wind,
And that destruction, too long without sound
Drifting beneath your unsuspecting feet,
Is a more terrible and utter end
Than any building fallen into sand
Being more tense and from a harder power
More deeply doomed.
                    Only last night I saw,
Vision or dream or madness of the eyes,
The whole world darken and on all the hills
The vague, bowed forms of kneeling men appear
One with the earth and night, their heads upturned
To the dim sky where light was less than light
Yet not so black as the broad hills, their hands
Thrust to the shoulders in the yielding earth.
Although the sky's brute weight was on their face
Some power in it pulled their sight above
And yet the earth drew their arms under it
Until the body like a tautened rope
Cried agony and could not rise or fall.
Then in their midst a slow gray light flared up
Quivering in the dark, and suddenly
The form and face of Christ burned on the world,
The lean face radiant where through its veins
Not blood but lightning ran and tore the heart,
The eyes bent and staring without sight,

BREAK THE HEART'S ANGER

Broken with looking at a human world,
Two thousand years bearing its jagged mass
In pity on the delicate thin lens.
The feet had sunk a little in the hill.
He lifted up his hands and moved them over
The crouching men in one long gesture not
Alone above them but above the world,
Blessing all things, the simple air they touched,
Then turned and from His leaning back tore off
The bitter cross, worn smooth with so long bearing,
And with one last wild waving of a hand
Wrote with its point along the trampled earth:

Here standeth my last will and testament.
All grace and pain I give to the world's children.
Kindness to birds. Property have I none
But a small house of faith and that I burn.
The sun's warmth and the moon's dark ease of
        madness
And all the force and fury of the earth,
The terrible necessity of growth
Out of the torn seed writhing with a cry
Into the clamor of created life,
The rain's sweetness and the wind's wide strength,
That last long benediction of the sky,
The light, the morning and the evening glow,
The midnight's graver shadow, the noon's glare,
The light—let it not tear your eyes away—
Water to be a coolness on the face,
All these I give to men, I give them back,
And the round earth to be a sort of home

NOTRE DAME

Long as it turn its white face with black hair
Forever shyly from the groping sun.
I go not from, now, but into the world,
And leave it for all men, they would not have
My own world in the sky or in their hearts
And so I give it back again with only
Their own wild human mood to comfort them.
But this one truth I write:

                             Though earth and all
Men resolve into one narrow ray
Of starlight and go hurtling off through space
Never to be the shape of life again,
Yet deeply blent on the Veronica
Handkerchief that is the cloth of time
Will be the immortal dreaming face of man,
All human moods that bless and curse him, all
Expressions of a nature never one
But multitudinous as the gnarled mind
Furiously mingled in one face
That will stare out eternity, its mouth
Twisted with human wailing and with laughter—
Because that unimaginable cloth
Had, in the doomed day of his agony,
Touched his dark tears and all the salty sweat
And gave him for a moment a gray peace.

The wind climbed and the kneeling men turned up
Their heads without delight, without despair,
Then bent them down and sank into the earth.
The light darkened and the dreaming Christ
Stood for a balanced instant on the wind

BREAK THE HEART'S ANGER

Before he dropped, clutching the dulled cross,
Into the quiet earth and night closed down
Leaving but blackness and infinity
And blowing from the gloomy wind where Christ
Had hung, the mournful fragment of a song:

Throttle the clocks and wring
The neck of time until
No enduring mood
Of human madness will
Hear what I must sing—

From this hour on the world
Moves a different thing,
No more round it curled
God's hands all slenderly
But the enormous wing
Of simple wind that we
Wandering on the ground
With little human cries
Break into our breath,
Too lonely, having found
Here on earth where lies
Our living, no dark death
Blinder than our eyes.

Today I saw a street,
One curving length of stone
Where men and women meet
Laid like a little bone
On earth's huge skeleton,

NOTRE DAME

At the lithe joint of a town
Where all the bent and broken
Men of the world walked down
With no word cried or spoken,
And there in the world's full sight
Begged for the food and bed
That are a man's full right
Being a man, the bread,
The huddled warmth at night,
And then—O world cry out
Shame's immortal shout,
Let not the thin throat tarry—
I saw with awful light
That every man was Christ
And every woman Mary.

Paris

BELLEAU WOOD

☆

AND SO AT LAST America came back.
Having looked so long at the enormous West
It heard the intolerable horns of war
And turning found with all a child's surprise
That there were men and nations to the east.
But in that brief look straight into the sun
The eyes were blinded and the brain struck mad.

I was just another of the boys joined up
Because the khaki uniforms were nice
And there were songs and music and some guy
With a loud mouth had told us we were lucky
To have this noble chance to save the world.
That Alexander and his ragtime band
Would march the honorable dead to heaven.
And so we came—the Swedes from Minnesota,
Blue blown out of the sky into their eyes,
The hunkies from the steel towns, all the Slavs
That couldn't learn commands but fought like hell,
The Ghetto Kikes who missed their koshered meat
And cussed the salt pork out in Yiddish, Wops
Who loved the Virgin Mary and the girl
At the cigar store with an equal passion,
And millions like me, had a decent job,
A steady girl, a Ford, on Saturdays

[161]

BREAK THE HEART'S ANGER

Went to a dance and Sunday morning slept,
With no hate for a country I'd not seen,
Couldn't have told a Froggie from a Hun,
But all the other boys were lining up
So I did too.
               It is a strange thing now
To feel how restlessly the bones live out
Unfinished life. Here in the valley where
The lithe creek writhes through fields made doubly
    fertile
With earth's most nourishing and nervous rain
That fell from us into the eager ground,
The blue-smocked peasants reap the grain with
    scythes
Whose strokes cut through me here, remembering
The Colorado plain and the long wheat.
So like our fathers in the windy West
We found a patch of land and paid our life.
Yet the rain's taste is like American rain
And from this little distance under earth
The sun is no more angry and the moon
Moves through its phases in no other way
Than when it climbed along the Rockies' edge
And dropped into the prairie. If a man
Must take his little dreaming under earth
Where idiot day can no more mock it, shrieking
Its violent laughter of the livid light,
This valley is as good a place as any,
But now the heart must break at evening
Hearing the homeward children on the road
Shouting the words he cannot understand,

BELLEAU WOOD

The little scraps of song, the running games,
And birds whose crying is a stranger thing.
Yet here deep under is my doom. I take it.
One man's life is over.
                              But if they come
To you mumbling in their moldy throats
That we have glory, honor or a peace
Or that their God will take us to His house
And that will be a greater thing than all
The women we have never touched, the hours
Of contemplation when the lonely mind
Hangs like a mote in moonlight and the winds,
The myriad lights of heaven and that inner
Radiance that is a more than light,
The mood and mystery of the lone self,
Wander around it till it is aware
Only of the tense energy of life
Not trembling, not with the breath's shudder nor
Even the heart's beat, but the enduring
Dream and image of our life, hurl back
The jagged words into their empty eyes
And hang them with the tough rope of their
        tongues.
If they say one brief word above us here
The total gathered yell of men who died
In all the hideous and howling ways
A human or wolf voice can rip the sky,
Or in a gasping quiet, the teeth clenched
In one white slavering and gritted grin,
Or crying "Mutter" in a scared child's voice,
Will break against their ears and through the head

BREAK THE HEART'S ANGER

Clamor and clang till echo breaks on echo
And the brain quiver, not to hear again.
Merchants in misery, dealers in despair,
Who feared your markets or a square of land
Stolen in some far corner of the world,
Makers of armaments, all you who sat
In the cursed chair of government and watched
The leaping conflagration in the eyes
Of men flare up before it took the world
Yet would not act, or only with shrill words,
Know that the flowing lava of our pain
Will harden to gray granite in your hearts,
The fluent agony that through our nerves
Flowed more irresistibly than tide
Will be a grim and durable enough
Monument on which to scratch your name.
With that contempt which is a greater thing
Than any hate, with quiet tongue, I speak,
Having no love but for the man who killed me
And for his deadly hands.

                    I also talk
With the same tongue to you who are another
People, a new world, born with the bitter
Taste of our world's failure in your mouth.
Here I have lain and watched the pale earth writhe
Sick of an old wound, the fever of it,
Seen the first day that your eyes bore the light
Like living flame thrust through them and your
    skin
Burned with the biting acid of the air.
Yet I have learned so little, only death,

BELLEAU WOOD

That is the one hard thing I understand.
It was not death that was my final doom
No larger than my childhood fear of night
Nor greater than the human curse of dream,
But it was living in a time when men
Held the heart no more than week-old meat,
A little rotten round the edge and fit
Only to be given to the dogs.
This I have found—living is a man
With calloused fingers quick to make a fist,
To strike what halt or hinder in its way,
And will give only angered restlessness.
Death is a woman with calm eyes and hands
Softer than the wavering touch of time
Who comes more naked than the simple light
To touch your face and give you from deep breasts
The white rich milk of her perpetual peace.
But lying here where change is more than change,
Is the progression and the pulse of earth,
I have felt new roots break soil and batter rock
And watched time grow big bellied with the future.
From here I call to you:
                              Quick now, before
The wind of sense blowing to the mind
Has moved so long across the tiring nerves
That the hands dull with what they touch and you
Are deafened with ears, blinded by your eyes,
And the heart hunger only for its pain,
Act while the iron of your will is hot
Burning the brain. O let your living be
The deep repudiation of our blood

BREAK THE HEART'S ANGER

To straighten what we twisted. In the world's
Booming blackness hang a little light,
The shining of your eyes. Although the sun
Bring to the earth only a deeper dark,
Its broad glare dropping one terrific shadow
Bruising the weary head, it is no end.
Be comforted with hope. Know a man may
With one struck match put out the moon and
    stars
Yet only for as long as the match burns.
We dead have found the past and other men
Will take the future but you have the now.
This is your heritage ripped for an hour
From the hard fingers of eternity.
Deep in the prism of your dreaming life
Take it, and as edged glass gives back the light,
The same lean rays bent to another way,
Hurl it far out.
              And think a day of us,
Of all the hate and greed that put us here,
Of how the human groveling for gold
So yellowed the immortal sight of men
They were content to pile before their banks,
Their private wealth, their markets, stocks and
    bonds,
The bodies of eight million men, the life
Cut out of them, the heart gouged from the breast.
And the uncounted millions that are ghosts,
The pulse yet beating but the man not there,
The maimed and blind, the twisted in the head,
Stretched on the agonizing rack of earth,

[166]

BELLEAU WOOD

The nails of wind and sun pierced through their
    eyes,
Who haunt the waste and welter of the world
That will not see or hear them, having built
Another golden wall before its face.
Think one day of us, and our strange names
Carved in this rock—Pietro Pisacretto,
Mike Abbott, Patsey Gullo, Junior Smith
The little bugler, Joe Zak, Christ Veagules,
Willie Day, Walt Adams, Ike Goldberg,
From all lands gathered in America
Then driven back without the right to die
In the new earth they had too soon called home.

We beg you now, let the mind take that mood
Compounded equally of dream and iron
That will no longer let the lust for gold,
The savage childlike yearning after power,
The madness of all men to hide their lives
Beneath a pile of sticks and stones and those
Material creations of the hands
Desperately crushing from the kind
Heart all gentleness in the cruel will
To make it tower higher than another's—
O generosity like autumn harvest
That will give all men all the earth for home,
The strength of mind that will not once a week
Sing peace on earth, good will to man, and six
Days rob and sweat him, goad him on to war,
But will let each man do his work in peace.
Now you have seen, America, the world

BREAK THE HEART'S ANGER

Drop through shuddering space but you, so young,
Can fall as a cat, or rather like your trained
Football player, lightly, without bones,
And rise uninjured to run on again
With a new power driving in your legs.
And we will rise to give you with a cry
The pity tender in our fingertips
Against the grief and barriers to come.
Give us no thanks unless you say of one
Without name huddled in the unnamed earth,
He could find thrushes in the gloomy night,
Once he was kind to a dog, water and leaf
He loved to touch.
                Poor sons of sorrow, come
More innocent than light into the world,
Who would have been by now the nicknamed
    friends
Of all the sons that we have never had,
Your eyes will crack as ours to see one night
Christ like a spear hurled in the hung earth's side.

It is a hard straight language that you speak,
America, full of tough ways a man
Can sink his teeth in like a hungry dog.
I come to you now with your own hard words.
We had our dreams, and then we marched across
The open wheatfields to the waiting wood
That suddenly broke out in hell and flame
And the gold wheat screamed redder than a heart
While that mad sergeant yelled, "Come on! Come
    on!

[168]

BELLEAU WOOD

You bastards, do you want to live forever?"
We the Marines, the picked and healthy men,
We took the wood, walking on our dead,
As the live future will one day on you
Step into its being. So we did
Our job and died, and the world called us brave.
But in that forest fighting, hand to hand,
We ground a bayonet with hating hands
Deep in the guts of twenty centuries
And at the hard hilt twisted it.

                                        O be
No longer an excited dream of God,
Tiny motes deep in His twitching eye,
But be your human self and that alone,
And with your mortal eager hands build up
Between Nantucket Light and Frisco Bay
A land that will be spirit, bone and blood
Of all its men, belonging to all men,
Not to a few who signed a bond for it,
Till living will be peace for them as calm,
As clear upon the face as light on stone,
And in the turning of the world, the swing
Of time outward to eternity,
It will be part of one enormous whole
Rich with the grain, the fruit, the light of earth,
And in an age when men will pity us,
The childlike stupid way in which we died,
Christlike you will walk upon the waters
Not of Bethsaida but of Michigan.

BREAK THE HEART'S ANGER

Until you act, until you make your living
What I have said, my voice will cry to you:

I who have borne
The double weight,
Under the earth,
Over the air,
Felt the heart torn
With double fate,
Cry to your birth
Without despair.

I am in your blood,
Will give you help,
Will drive you on
Though the breath wail—
The horse's thud,
The eagle's yelp,
Will break the sun
Before you fail.

Cry in the night
For fear of dark,
Beat the noon's light
Being too stark,
Wherever you go
You will have found,
Winter on snow,
Summer on ground,
Where the wind blow
I will be your hound.

Achensee, Tirol

ATLANTIC PASSAGE—WEST

☆

Migrating bird forever to the west
Beating with golden wings, on what long flight
Out of the hollow dawn? In the dark thrust
And backward reach of time what autumn chill
Called to you beyond the crying air
Till with one final climb, loud with singing,
You wheeled above the old and fiery nest
And hurled off westward? What terrific bough
Waits you in that far land where time no more
Tinctures the wind with the red hue of change
And through the leaves on the wide tree of light
Clambers the future on its gripping claws
To mate with you and fling out to the stars
Wild and wailing fledglings winged of flame,
With eyes of anger?
                    Nothing of this I know,
But only that, the rivers and wrought peaks,
Volga, Dnieper, Danube and the Rhine,
Loire, the often bloodied Marne, the Thames,
Watzmann, Jungfrau and the Matterhorn,
Wrinkles and lines on the broad brain of Europe,
The nerves of men and all their huge excitement,
The blood cry bellowed on the radio,
The maimed at Lourdes, the countless crippled
    minds

[173]

BREAK THE HEART'S ANGER

That took the knife between the ribs where song
Had fluttered once, the edge of Brittany
Where the pale Iseult lingers in the foam,
All these left clear behind, the snarling water,
You touch, the great feet trailing darkness here,
Your glaring wings wide out from pole to pole,
The face and heart of men who are my people,
A width of earth that is familiar land
Where a child's games were played and a speech
    known
Quick on the tongue and sight first walked the
    mind,
Hands felt hard metal and a woman's hair
And huddled in the dark:
                There have been
So many good-byes with America on the lips,
Hope or despair beating in the heart,
The thought of home falling through the mind
More cold than autumn rain, through the first
    night.
And now I add another—with a patched
Emigrant bundle, shirts and a few dreams,
A pair of socks, the words for living strange,
I sail away into the friendless West.
Was it America Ulysses felt
Hiding, the hills not burdened with a Troy,
Behind the twilight sun?
               The lean grim face
Of New York breaking through the morning mist
Above North River with bright nervous eyes
And loud mouth shouting while it stares into

ATLANTIC PASSAGE—WEST

Atlantic waves and breathes the clean salt wind
That runs through the drilled rows of stone, the tall
Cornfields of buildings where no crickets chirp.
Then the two bodies of America—
East the Empire State, the hard male thrust
Into the light, direct and clear and simple
Like one straight wisdom of our mind; beyond
The female prairie with the fertile earth
Lying full length, the Mississippi back
Curled a little with the wide-flung arms,
Missouri and Ohio, gripping fingers
On mountain ranges half a world apart,
The brown feet splashing in the friendly Gulf,
Giving with supple body and deep breasts
The continent's eternal recreation.
Lonely and lithe American body, now
Let the rats have you and the naked buzzards
Tear their blood-cruel beaks into your heart
Seeing you are more noble and more wise
Than any human life that swarms you here,
Crouching beneath your arms to hide the cold,
Knowing only the remorseless hands
White against their throat, against their breath,
In the long strangulation of no job,
While all your richness and fertility,
The kindliness of crops under the sun,
The strength in corn that is like the earth's power
Of plunging through the stars become a life,
Given green leaves and roots and thirst for rain,
Are issued out in packets—if you beg
Or swear you have less home than alley rats

[175]

BREAK THE HEART'S ANGER

With nests beneath the barn.

                                    We have always
Had the hard-boiled cadgers, the old-timers
Who'd made a racket of it all their lives,
The tramps and hobos who in any time
Would have been the moochers with the snarling
    whine,
The scorning bums who hopped the fastest freights,
The fly-by-nights riding the rods to hell,
The down-and-outers scared of death and work,
The restless hands tracking the harvest north,
All wanderers along the continent
From Lake of the Woods plumb south to Rio
    Grande,
From Puget Sound eastward to Cape Fear,
Inheritors of wind and hills for home,
The railroad jungle and the can of stew,
The westward moving of a nation fled
Into their blood, the last Americans
Going forever onward without end
Fearing but the black ash of last night's fire,
To sleep in the same bed, a steady job,
Forty-niners of the railway ties
Or hitting the highway with a hard-luck yarn.
These are of the land, they are a part of it.
But all the millions who are on the street,
Only a few years footloose—wandering
From town to town and corner to street corner,
The trained minds loafing on the curb or taking
Jobs a kid could do, at a kid's wage,
Youngsters just out of school, the men with hands

ATLANTIC PASSAGE—WEST

Quicker than thought, skillful at long-learned
    trades,
These are the tough reality, it is
Their voice that cries at night:
                        Will you never
Know honest truth that slaps you in the face
But call it fallen leaf or only wind?
We are the midstream rock, splitting the current,
Bearing the flood upon our breast, our heart,
Until we break away, until we break.
America, are you content to live
An old Ford rattling on through history?
It's not much that we want, a little earth,
The chance to work it, and a house for sleeping.
This is our land, our people, and they want,
Gnawing a crust when the ripe wheat is burned.
They wrote a paper once that said a man
Had his right to life, to liberty,
To happiness—but do you call this life,
This begging for too little warmth and bread?
What liberty is here but that of dying?
What happiness but getting for a day,
With luck, the dirtiest of makeshift jobs?
It is a simple thing we want, the right
Of working for our life when we are young,
A decent quiet when we grow too old.
Rewrite those words or burn them in the street
Little brittle autumn leaves. Unless you do,
We shall, and the letters will be red.
Once again, and for the same old cause,
The humble rights of humble men, will fly

[177]

BREAK THE HEART'S ANGER

The proud banner of American blood,
And once more through the river-sinewed land
A newer life will tremble and take shape
To startle the world's eyes.

                        Now you belong
Not to a continent but to that world.
You gave it one dream, have you not another?
One hundred and fifty years ago you showed
The full way out and the earth followed, now
Cry from some Alleghany height to it:

No, I will not be Virgil, lead you down
Through the dark underworld and that deep river,
But Sacajawea, Bird Woman of the mountains,
To guide you through the peaks that tear the sun,
The valleys where the grass comes first, the dry
Canyons with the hidden water holes,
Through all the country of today, the West
That is a mood of mind, a way of life.
I come to you now out of your own heart,
One with the world's deep-chambered heart that
     beats
With the terrific pulse of centuries,
To tell you of the land beyond, the fields
Where grass in June is high as a tall man,
Where deer run through the timber like great birds,
Where over beaches never cut by ships
An ocean booms and fish leap through the wind.
Auto cannot be driven nor plane land,
You must take the unblazed footway on fierce rock

[178]

That will burn through the foot and break the
    hand,
But in that air of morning you will find
A newer love you have not dared or dreamed,
Another living no more like your own
Than flame is like the shadow that it casts,
And a new way of dying, a new death.

Go up, America, to some high place,
Bad Lands, Big Horns or the Cascade Range,
And with the light of time against your eyes
Draw back the hickory tough bow of the world
Strung with the finest deer gut and fling out
Between the glowing wolf eyes of the stars
The hard lean shafted arrow of a man,
Feathered with dream and tipped with the flint
    mind.

Drifting back to earth the arrow's cry:

    I who am soil and history,
    The daring blood, and what men know
    Of all that was and is to be,
    With a rock's touch and the wind's curve
    Balanced sure and fashioned clear
    By light above and dust below,
    Roped and tied like a thrown steer
    With the supple lariat of nerve,
    I the tanned bulldogger, taking
    The bronco earth between my thighs
    With sheepskin chaps and steel spurs raking

BREAK THE HEART'S ANGER

The sweating sides until they rise
To crash the fence and bang their feet
In time's corral, lined with the eyes
Of men and suns who raise their cries,
"Ride 'im, cowboy, till he's beat."

And I will ride him out where stars
Are thick on the sky like golden sand,
And burn on his hide the double bars
Filled with a face, that is my brand.
No more, an untamed maverick,
Will he jump the massive gate of light,
Piled with oak a man's arm thick,
To neigh in the mate-desiring night.
Though the flesh quiver and the nose
Snarl, I will make him bear a pack
Till bit and bridle are things he knows
And the saddle no more galls his back.
But never till the spirit goes,
The kicking lust to take the track,
To leave the valley fields and climb
The last plateaus and peaks of time,
And neigh to the stallion sun at noon
Or night to that dark mare the moon.

Haüsern, Black Forest

EPILOGUE AT THE CORE
OF EARTH

Here at the axle of the earth I stand
And turn with its slow turning while I take
Upon my back the driving power that holds
Suns and planets in the hollow sky
Unwavering against the wind of space
Blowing like winter's anger from a north
Beyond the vision or the eye of mind,
And I can feel eternity flow through
My arteries until its beat is one
With the wrist's pulse and echoes in the heart.
Here I call through fire and rock and root
To the world's men:
                              You lengths of talking wind
Breaking hill and stone between your hands
After the Moses rod of the sunlight
Touched rock and, living water, you leapt forth.
As fire moves outward from the depth of stars,
Being the shape and body of their life,
Are you the glow and radiance of earth.
O happy, happy dust doomed but to dream
Into the word and figure of a man—
Skeleton patched up with stubborn bone,
Muscle intricately woven over,
Nerve striding through the flesh like flame,
Blood beating like a flight of wings

BREAK THE HEART'S ANGER

Through the great sky of heart, the wind of vein,
Feet that walk and make a mark on grass,
Arms that reach beyond the sun, that hold
A breathing body in them, hands carved out
From eagerness, the writhing mood of touch,
Two sills of eyes worn with the sight's walking
Back and forth between the world and brain,
With all the faces moving over it,
The deep hollows where the light has run,
And back of them, coiled in a hollow sphere,
Harder, a little, than sea chalk, the mind,
Ultimate strange ecstasy of earth
Being touchable hard matter and yet ghost.

Here is the final act and power of rock
Threshed into the dreaming chaff of dust,
Word and wonder of the tangled forms
Huddled on bark or thrust into the air,
Creeping in swamps or running over wheat,
Gliding through water, burrowed in a leaf,
The will and way of living in one tense
Grip of human mood and substance blent,
Flame mingling with the wood it burns.
Mind that holds the known and unknown stars,
Color of clouds and eyes and gray stone moss,
Sound of birds and talk and beaten iron,
Smell of weather in the wind and clothes,
Taste of brown bread, bacon and dark beer,
Touch of sun on hair and cold and hands,
Force that by the chemistry of thought
Can fuse from these a new, more shining thing.

EPILOGUE AT THE CORE OF EARTH

And in one corner where the echo cries
Memory of the past like a lean spider
Crouches in the gray web of time and draws
Out of its belly recreated life.
Moving madness of a solid stuff
Bewitched, haunted or inhabited
By troubled spirits vaguer than the air
That hide in the brain's crevices but crawl
In sleep to steal the eyes and be themselves
More real than sight. Little world of dream
Holding all worlds.
            This multitude
Of sense and bone and will and the blood's anger
Gathered in one tormented, gasping life.
This dignity and terror of the dust,
No more a beast than it is less a god.
This bend of ribs around a yell of wind
Making a word. This man who wears the earth
For coat, not with an anxious pride but humbly
Knowing it is his larger self and he
Its trembling heart.
            He who has two names,
Man and spirit—if one shape of sound
Over the tongue can utter what he is,
This fury of hard matter hung in light,
Those two quick words are one—man like a breath
Cries from the mouth of time, being one wild
Wandering ghost until the echo dies.
Man is a spirit. Look upon his face
Or in his eyes or take him by the hand.
O spiritual mood of simple earth,

BREAK THE HEART'S ANGER

From deep in the maddened marrow of your bones
I call to you:
           The days and centuries
Move through the light. You are no more a child.
Until this moment life has carried you
But now your memory is full of years,
The hands are tough, and you must carry life,
Wading rivers, crossing busy streets,
Keeping the bitter wind and rain away,
The chin leaned forward like a driving wedge
Into the future, with one eye the gull's
To watch through water and one eye the hawk's
To stare through space. Take with your mind's
    sight
The knowledge and the need that is your life:

You are the watershed of history.
Time falls on you and splits and down one side
Runs back into the past through the old ways,
The deep channels and the gullied fields,
To the dark tides that through a moonless night
Break on the changing beaches of the sun,
And down the other, sprawling on deep rock,
In no carved watercourse but everywhere
The granite future cracks and drops off sheer,
Into the tideless depth of time to come,
That unedged ocean running from your eyes
Out to infinity, whose end is one
Endless wave and then another wave,
Water beyond green water and no wind.

Your feet are shadow but your face is light.

EPILOGUE AT THE CORE OF EARTH

Will you not know it? Have you never watched
A swallow flying, black until it wheeled
And the sun flashed its belly white? Look up.
The massive bird that beats the west wind down
With wings made each of a hundred feathers, turns
In flight, and now there is another time.

This will be called the century of fire.
You think you live in darkness. It is flame
So bright it blinds your eyes, your staring mind.
But soon, Monday, perhaps, on a new week
You will see the world on fire and shout in fright
Until you know you are yourself that flame
And what you think the fire's heart is your own
Life blooded heart burned fiercely from your breast
And down the world's streets running with loud
    tongue,
A voice more cry than word, more song than cry.

Here between your hands the limp earth lies
Weary two thousand years with carrying
A mourning, broken man upon its back,
The torn feet trailing and the arms stretched out,
The poor hands groping but to find a spike,
The bitter vinegar upon his mouth
Twisted into a word's shape strange for us
Who know no more its meaning or its mind,
Yet it was only "Father" that it cried.
So it will lie, the bones bent, till you give
Your living up, to be a life for it,
The long transfusions ended and your blood

BREAK THE HEART'S ANGER

Beating through the broad arteries of rock,
The face no longer pale but like a star
Breaking the night.
                              If you have not the strength
Of thought, or hard endurance of your nerve
To give it a new life, lift up your hands
And let it drop through bellowing black space
Till a sun's anger burn it or it burst
With too far falling.
                              No terrific work
A man could do more difficult than this,
More dark with death. And yet it is not doom,
You are not cursed by it as by a fate
Hung in the vague of time to crack your eyes.
It is your blood right and your heritage,
Your power of living and your right of breath
Deeper in you than bone.
                              Although you are
Immortal man born of immortal earth,
Being but that, and all too human, know
That when the heart breaks so must break the
        mind.

No longer backward lean on the worn crutch
That is your shadow and will snap, nor cry
That the one way of life is to be born
Pitied by others till you pity them.
You must destroy before you can create,
It is the surest way beyond tomorrow.
No longer build up ruins out of ruins,
But break the old and wash your hands of it.

EPILOGUE AT THE CORE OF EARTH

In the despair of faith call not again
Life but a quick and curious way of dying.
In no night will the hardest sleep dream back
The hand of God again upon your face.
You will but wake to know more certainly
There is one truth, the simple truth of living,
That the unresting fingers of quick change
Take away your house and gold, your hope
To live forever, leave but a thin coat
Against the winter, and yet you are rich
With nothing left at all, nothing but love.
Act, or in the mass that over you
The dancing light and all the laughing suns
Will chant with tongues of anger, will be burned
The leaping tapers of your cloud-flung towers.

Now the bare cry, "God is," no more can stop
The heart with awe or make the hair stand up,
Now men no longer feel upon their skin
The spirit of the living Lord like wind,
Nor the eyes break to watch the night come down
Knowing it is the shadow of a god,
Nor body tremble at the thought of Christ.
Now one full world is ended and its time.
You are the makers of another world,
You with your mortal hands.
                              Build with fire,
Desperation and blue tempered steel,
The durable, dark stone that is the mind,
Till the skyscrapers flower on their huge stalks,
Your eyes become but clear intensities

BREAK THE HEART'S ANGER

Mingled of starlight and the staring blood.
And at the lean nerve end of being tear
Tongues from bells and beat them with your hands
Till the world calls you mad, knowing you are
Men possessed and out of mind with life.

Now you live in a hard and iron time,
The clangor and the pound of mad machines
Crashing their brutal thunder in your brain
Split with the lightning of the radio—
Sons and workers of metallic bone
Out of your own red guts created. Fear
Not that like the saurians of old time
Or monsters in the marveling folk tales
They will roam cryingly through all the land,
Beat the night and batter down your door
To kill you with one scream. In the new world
That will be your own living, you will find
Wandering on the hills, talking to birds,
The proud-eyed prophets of the dynamo,
The saints of the machine.
                              Cry to all men,
This is another century, awake
Not by the gun of dawn or air alarm
But with the clangings of a brazen bell
That are triumphant beatings of your heart.

Unless you do, every uttered word
Will be your funeral dirge, sung by yourself.
The little children walk, their thin bones stained
With hunger till they startle through the skin.

[190]

EPILOGUE AT THE CORE OF EARTH

Once more have men drawn out the knife to shout
The names of Caesars in the bloodied streets,
And what were once proud, simple beings now
Are cursed with the name of man.

                           O work in wind,
In water, in gray rock that once beneath
Oceans crawled and had its own tough life,
In the gaunt mind, until the world at last
And for the first time move through space as one
Turn and power and song of dreaming men,
The bent and bitter symbol of their lives
Carved and gashed with their despairing hands,
Echoing with their deadly cries but loud
With a clear call into the future, dark
No more with the wild multitude of hate,
For love in the kind night will like the moon
Touch the world with dark and gentle fire.
But if you fail, but if you fail, then know
The pitiless eyes of your posterity
Will haunt your dying and will say of you,
Brutus generation on your swords
Self-hurled—O Strabo, hold it hard and turn
Your face away—it is a nobler death
Than any you deserved.

                        Here I will lie
At the earth's axle till it crack and rock
Resolve into original, bare light,
But hear my voice:

                    Neither Utopia
Nor the white heaven you have sung I speak,
But a hard human world made by its men

BREAK THE HEART'S ANGER

Into a place where living is not pride,
Neither long sorrow nor a battered head,
But only human strength and hope and thought
Mingled in one acceptance, one creation,
One unity of brain and bone and earth
Tempered with moonlight, bent beneath the wind,
The restless hands like autumn-driven birds
Imploring but to touch a speaking face,
Comfort the troubled eyes, the friendly mouth.

Lean heart of man, born for tragedy,
Doomed but to break. Tender, believing heart
Hungry for nothing more than a small faith,
Must you time and time with never peace
Watch one portion of your blood flow out,
The long-known and familiar beat of wrist,
And feel the struggle, the deep agony
When the new blood from every nourished part
Of the worn body flows to the blue veins?
Is there a mood of twenty centuries
That moves through earth and wanders in the wind
And is instinctive to the minds of men
As touch to fingers, till another mood
Breaks through the sky and in the brain goes mad?
One great cycle of all human thought,
One thudding, sunlight-driven wheel of change
On which the hollow bones of men are broken?
Two thousand years from now what other dream
Will run along the beaches of the world
In the coiled noose of angry foam that creeps
Around the throat of every continent,

EPILOGUE AT THE CORE OF EARTH

To leap up in the land and with no pity
Hang the neck of man?

                    Yet who am I,
A lone man bitter that his head is tired,
His heart's old anger broken by its grief
Until the unrelenting tongue cry out—
Mind, beat not the undesiring blood,
Pale will, find another peace than death,
Hand, be gentler on loved face than light—
Who am I to speak against the wind,
Driving my lost words down it like wild ducks?
Though I have wandered over road and world,
Walking the plowed fields like the sea of Christ,
Have I found out the deep and shape of earth,
Knowing it move along the mind like thought,
That I dare call to any man, Oh break
The right hand so the left may live and carve
Your name in granite with your own thigh bone?

Yet I have talked day-long to men, their mouths
Hungry for the taste of simple words,
Friend and hope and food—Quai Malaquais,
The Seine beneath us quicker than our feet;
Potsdamerplatz, hands before our lips
Hiding the exiled words; the Kärntnerring,
Machine guns huddled in the trees like birds;
Tenderloin, the Bowery and Harlem,
Cops with clubs—Shove along there, buddy,
Pick 'em up and put 'em down a long way off.
And in dark alleys I have knelt and stroked

BREAK THE HEART'S ANGER

The desolate glad heads of dogs, their bark
Eager with fear.
                    Shall I not answer them?

But it is hard—how can I know the earth,
The touch of rock, the tenderness of men,
Madness of nation or the mood of leaf,
The yell of time forever at my ear,
When waking in the night my worn hands shudder
To feel my body burn them like lean flame,
When eyes can stare farther than stone be thrown
But never look one thin hair's breadth behind
In the intolerable glare of brain
Where self is vaguer and less touchable
Than wind not seen, not gripped, but crying there?

And yet a man must say—here is the hard
Ground I walk, these are the groping words
That on light-padded feet howl through my mind,
Snarling to rip the throat of every thought
But never closer than a track in sand,
Here is my heart talking:
                        You who are
Madness and fury of the living earth,
Now when the weary head that is the world
Hangs in space, tired with long history,
While the immortal hands of day and night
Give it the sun for warmth, the moon for sleep,
Comfort it like a child on time's broad breast,
Live till every sense and the quick mind
Are more aware of life than eyes of light,

EPILOGUE AT THE CORE OF EARTH

Till you know that rivers and Orion's stride,
The broken autumn leaf and Mars' red hate,
A fish hawk's plunge, the lifting of your hand,
The wind's flight and the walking of your feet,
Are one, self-blooded, and that drawing breath
Is faith and eating food a holy act.

Until the individual no more
Lonelier than earth alone in space
Cries to his livid nerves.
                     Then shall the mind
Take from its dreaming wildness and its wrath
Repose in fury, fury in repose,
And while the whole world blooms like a pale
    flower,
Carved the deep petal from the rock of earth,
Shall, in every valley and on hills,
Warm in men's hands and eager in their eyes,
The act of living be the act of loving.

Achensee, Tirol